# RAISE YOUR RIGHT HAND AGAINST FEAR

*Extend
the Other
in Compassion*

# Sheldon Kopp

BALLANTINE BOOKS • NEW YORK

Passages from Heinrich Zimmer's *The King and the Corpse* reprinted by permission of Princeton University Press.

Library of Congress Catalog Card Number: 88-19900

ISBN 0-345-36624-7

This edition published by arrangement with CompCare Publishers.

Manufactured in the United States of America

First Ballantine Books Edition: April 1990

Praise for
# RAISE YOUR RIGHT HAND AGAINST FEAR

"Sheldon Kopp has done it again! His freedom to open his heart and the intimacy of his professional world teases me to dare a deeper look at my own world. Greater love is rare in any man. His awareness of death and his subtle version of self-other have almost unlimited power."

CARL WHITAKER, M.D.
Co-author of *The Family Crucible*

"The intriguing case studies and poignant self-disclosure contained in this book will provide readers with countless pathways with which to explore the profoundest and scariest of their emotions. For the depth of his unforgettable insights we owe Kopp an enormous debt and a thorough reading."

GERALD AMANDA, Ph.D.
Author of *A Guide to Psychotherapy*

"In *If You Meet the Buddha on the Road, Kill Him!*, therapist Kopp tackled the subject of personal responsibility; here he turns his attention to inner and outer fears, arguing that only by facing them head-on can one dare to risk vulnerability and compassion.... Persuasive."

*Library Journal*

All accounts of patients are disguised to protect their privacy. In some instances, the portraits I have presented are composites. In others, identifying biographical details have been either omitted or changed.

# Contents

# Prologue

Determined to destroy the Buddha, a dark and treacherous demon unleashed an elephant charging drunkenly. Just as the wildly raging beast was about to trample him, the Buddha raised his right hand with fingers held close together and open palm facing the oncoming animal. The fearless gesture stopped the elephant in its tracks and completely subdued the recklessly dangerous creature. Once having faced the terrible threat of annihilation, the compassionate Buddha extended his other hand with its palm up, as if cupping the offering of an open heart. This selflessly charitable gesture of forgiveness restored the elephant's natural tranquility.

The Sanskrit word for such ritually symbolic gestures is *mudra*.[1] The Buddha's first mudra allowed him to face the fears in his own momentarily uncontrolled imagination. Having turned back the terror that threatened him from without, he was able to address his attention to the horror harrowing the elephant from within. Only after having eased his own anxiety, was the Buddha then free to confer on the elephant a benevolent second mudra of compassion that calmed the bewildered beast.

Although, like the psychotherapist and other contemporary gurus, the Buddha may have nothing to teach, as patients and disciples we all have much to learn. If we wish to overcome our cautions and feel safe enough to risk trusting others in caring ways, we must learn how to face our fears.

One

# Safety and Danger

## 1

# Feeling Afraid Can Sometimes
# Keep Us Safe from Harm

When I was a child, my parents dismissed all of my own personal fears as silly. Meanwhile they insisted that whatever made my mother anxious was an actual danger that I had to avoid at any cost.

My mother designated anything she found unfamiliar as an aspect of life I was to fear as harmful. Even non-Jewish foods made her nervous: "You never know what the *Goyim* (Gentiles) put into what they eat." Because of their popularity in Jewish neighborhoods, chow mein and pizza were allowed as inexplicably safe exceptions.

Our family's other central catastrophic fear was loss of control. Understandably alarming excesses (such as violence) had to a be kept in check, and enthusiasm as well. "Too much excitement is not good," she told me. "You think you're just having fun, but sooner or later someone is sure to get hurt."

Whenever I played hard as a child, my mother warned me, "Don't get wild. You'll take out somebody's eye." I was never allowed to ride a bike, and it took some time to convince my parents that I would be safe learning how to rollerskate. Because they were frightened when I showed any sign of being adventurous, they condemned my independent displays of enthusiasm as "inconsiderate." I was ten years old before they believed that I could be careful enough to own a pair of roller skates.

I behaved then as I still occasionally behave now. My shyness and constraint were punctuated by episodes of absolute recklessness. On my tenth birthday, I broke loose on my new skates. I took off on a steep, block-long hill without being at all sure just how I would stop once I reached the bottom.

The faster I went the better I liked it. I had just begun to worry about how the trip would end when my attention focused on the corner lamppost at the bottom of the hill. I envisioned myself making a last-minute grab for the post and swinging round to a graceful halt.

I miscalculated. Rather than catching the lamppost in the crook of my arm as I had hoped, I caught it full on the side of my face in an incredibly painful and frightening collision. Evidence of my shortsighted valor later appeared in the form of a super black eye and a severely injured jaw muscle.

For a while I just sat on the curb, crying as little as possible. By then, I was really scared. It was time to go home and face my mother. If not for that, I might well have experienced this unfortunate accident as no more than a minor mishap about which I could feel understandably shaken, somewhat sorry for myself, and entitled to sympathy. Instead, all I felt was that once again I would alarm my poor parents. Nervously slinging the new skates over my shoulder, I headed home and cautiously climbed the four flights of stairs to the family apartment.

I had to warn and reassure my mother before I could go in. Her reaction was completely predictable: "What now? Again you didn't stop to think about how much it upsets a mother to see a boy who is too wild to stay out of trouble!" I spent the next hour apologizing for my thoughtlessness and promising her that I would try to live a safer life. Ignoring the shock of my own scary experience, I attempted to ease my mother's anxiety about having a reckless son.

Even now, I hate how many moments of our lives we have to ignore our own feelings for the sake of indulging our anxieties and those of other people. In this book, I hope to offer readers an understanding of apprehensions they might otherwise ignore, so that they can learn to cope in ways that will open them to discovering new options for themselves.

I can't presume to tell anyone else how to be happy. As a writer and as a therapist, I can only help people to free themselves of unnecessary suffering. If we are to extend the trust and compassion needed to create close and caring relationships, first *we must learn to ease our anxieties by facing our fears.* Intimacy requires us to reveal our naked selves. How else can we put our hearts in another's hands?

Fear has been with us from the moment of our birth. What an alarming experience it must be for the startled newborn baby to be hurtled from the snug safety of the womb into a wildly unfamiliar outside world. As helplessly dependent infants, we felt frightened whenever danger appeared imminent, or protection was perceived as uncertain.

Growing up helped some. Most of us feel stronger and wiser as adults than we did as children. But even once we've grown up, there are still times when we encounter actual or imagined situations so appalling that we are filled with terror, and instances when we see aspects of ourselves so repelling that we are overcome with horror.

Even when our adult lives seem safe, we remain vulnerable to apprehension about experiences we have not yet had to deal with. How often we are haunted by the anxiety of the dreaded "What if (something terrible were to happen)?" An unexpected catastrophe could overtake any of us. No matter how well we take care of ourselves, who knows when we might get seriously ill? Or run over by an automobile? In the lottery of random accidents, any name can be drawn as today's unlucky victim.

We may consider ourselves to be decent, stable people. But no matter how well-intended and well-organized we may be, some unexpected stress might push us over the edge. Then we would have lost control even of ourselves.

Who among us is totally free of anxiety about our hidden craziness, or some secretly evil aspect, or a masked weakness in ourselves that might be revealed once we were out of control? We remain at risk all of our lives. None of us is completely safe from unexpected encounters with unforeseen misfortunes, or from making some ruinous mistake.

No one is ever totally safe from harm. No matter how cautiously we live our lives, occasionally we are injured. Sometimes we suffer sickness, and someday we are certain to lose someone or something we value dearly. The most deadly dangers are both universal and unavoidable. Inevitably, we all get sick, grow old, and die.

Even so, we need not always play it safe. We don't have to live constricted lives, anxiously clinging to familiar patterns that seem secure. Instead, it is possible to learn to face fears, find courage, indulge curiosity about the unknown, and to improvise a colorful and adventuresome life-style, all without putting ourselves needlessly and recklessly at risk. We need not remain too fearful to live life on our own.

Courage is not the absence of fear. It is the ability to face fear. Independence does not require living without support from others. It is the developed capacity to adequately care for ourselves instead of childishly clinging to others for protection. We can claim both courage and independence without unnecessarily endangering our safety. Being brave does not imply never backing off from danger, and attaining autonomy does not mean *never* counting on care from others to protect us from harm.

The willingness to risk can bring about otherwise unattainable rewards. If we choose to run scared, our capacities for adult love and compassion remain limited and undeveloped. Unless we are willing to move beyond feeling afraid of new experiences, and always depending on the safety provided by others, we dare not see other people as having separate selves of their own.

Instead we can only experience others as they relate to our own sense of security—either they threaten it or protect it. And when we cannot see people wholly separate from ourselves, we end up limiting our involvement with them to avoiding the danger of their disapproval, or seeking the seemingly secure safety of their approval.

Enjoyment of an adventuresome adult life requires that we learn to discriminate between false alarms and the real alarms that are reliable signals of jeopardy. We need to realize that attitudes acquired earlier for meeting childhood threats may turn out to be unsuited to defend against adult dangers.

Panic is the paralyzing anticipatory fear of being afraid. It is equivalent to standing at a threshold, and declaring that it is too difficult to cross simply because something we cannot bear to know about lies on the other side. Unless we learn not to panic, we cry before we've been hurt without permitting ourselves to pass into the uncharted territory of adventure, courage, curiosity, caring, and personal growth.

Before we try to move beyond our fears, however, it would be wise to begin by understanding those times when we need to honor our anxieties. Otherwise we might foolishly dismiss these safeguards just when we need them most. If we *never* experienced the restricting discomfort of the primitive emotion of fear, we would get hurt more often, and perhaps die sooner.

Feeling afraid is an awful experience, but often it is unwise to ignore the alarm that signals we are at risk. Fear does not always indicate that we face actual danger, nor does a sense of security serve as a sure sign that we are safe, but if we attend to occasions of dread with discernment, feeling afraid can sometimes keep us safe from harm without restricting our freedom.

When we fear harm from external danger, we feel an impulse to move *away from* threatening objects, and *toward* sources of safety. As infants, whenever we felt ourselves falling, we cried out and clung to anyone who would hold us. Our instinctual fear of the threat of injury and of the imminent loss of a safe haven, made us want to hang on to our mothers more tightly. This reaction to alarm alerted our mothers to hold us more securely. Repeated experiences like this gradually made us apprehensive and anxious, alerting us to fearful possibilities even before we had begun to feel ourselves falling.

Simply being held insecurely became a warning signal that we might be about to fall, and could hope to be protected. The fear felt so bad, and the relief of mother's protection so good, that anticipated danger was sometimes mixed with the exquisite anticipation of perfect safety. Some of us had mothers who did not gradually encourage our emerging capacities for taking care of ourselves. Eventually, because of the seductive promise of relief, we ended up addicted to anxieties we might otherwise have outgrown.

As we acquired apprehension about injury, our innate fear of falling gradually grew more complex. At the same time, we learned anxiety about loss of protection. In some of our childhood situations, these two types of fear were more distinctly divided. For example, as toddlers, when we were frightened by a barking dog, we withdrew apprehensively from the frightening animal, and anxiously approached a protective parent.

When the situation was as simple as finding ourselves between the dog on one side and mother on the other, our fear clearly directed our course of escape. If, however, we had to move past the dog to get to mother, or away from mother to distance ourselves from the dog, our situation was more complicated and our impulses more conflicting.

The child's fear of the barking dog is the prototype of adult *terror* of something unfamiliar in the external world that might harm us. *Apprehension* is our anticipation of being hurt. Fear of separation from the protective mother prefigures the adult *horror* of exposure of anything within ourselves awful enough to threaten rejection by those we depend on for safety. *Anxiety* is our dread of their abandoning us.

Sometimes terror and horror intertwine. The most frightening situation for a young child is the dreadful discovery that at times *mother is the barking dog*. That's what it was like for me, most of the time I was growing up. I was a battered child just as some of you were. Even those of us who did not suffer excessive physical abuse had times in our childhoods when we reached out to our mothers for comfort and instead received either an icy air of indifference, or an unexpected outburst of irritability.

Unless mother then recognized our alarm and restored the security of our relationship, we were too young, needy, and dependent to experience her indifference or irritability as anything other than a frightening rejection. At the time, she may have simply been too ill, exhausted, or upset to respond with the appropriately attentive care that she otherwise would have wished to offer us. But there was no way for us to understand how distracted mother felt. If she acted irritated, we may have felt afraid that she would hurt us. Even if she simply ignored us when we reached out to her, we took it to mean that we were unloved and consequently unsafe.

In my own childhood, I felt afraid that almost anything I did might upset my mother. She beat me often. At times I was terrified that she would never stop. Eventually, I experienced the horror of feeling that I was such an awful child that anyone who knew me would hate me and hurt me.

Sometimes my mother simply slapped me around, but more often she hit me with a wooden hanger, a metal spatula, or whatever happened to be at hand. She was deadly with a high-heeled shoe thrown from across the room. Although she sometimes threatened to buy a leather-thonged whip, a cat-o'-nine-tails like the one in my aunt's broom closet, I was grateful that she never did.

My fear of her frequent, unpredictable outbursts of seemingly uncontrollable rage kept me tense and vigilant. Her occasionally more deliberate, slow and steady twisting pinches scared me even more. I was happy that my father seldom got openly angry with me. The few times he spanked me were because I had upset my mother.

I hated living in a house where I was in constant danger of getting hurt, but I feared the future even more. My mother often assured me that she was the only one in the world who would ever put up with me, and that even she had her limits. She threatened that if I did not learn to behave myself and stop being bad, someday she would have to send me to reform school. I had recurrent nightmares that I would grow up spending the rest of my life locked up in prison.

As children, even if the only frightening situations we experienced were the simplest ones of a barking dog on one side and an attentive mother on the other, enough of these encounters with fear taught us to stay farther away from strange animals and closer to familiar family members. With fear, apprehension, and anxiety as our teachers, we learned how to cope with the threats that frequently upset us.

As a result of these childhood experiences, some of us became excessively fearful. Unfortunately, for some of us this excessive fearfulness remains a way of life well beyond the time we need it. We go on uneasily avoiding unfamiliar activities by hiding out in routine patterns of behavior aimed at ensuring the protective approval of other people. As a result, we may feel secure, but our timid lives are terribly dull. We worry so much about what might happen next that, in the interest of avoiding the pain of shock, we end up sacrificing the pleasure of surprise.

The restrictions imposed by fear may not be confined to simply acting well-behaved, avoiding extraordinary events, and missing out on opportunities to enjoy ourselves. Worse yet, fearing that even our unexpressed thoughts and feelings may somehow expose us to danger, we will not even allow ourselves the private luxury of boldly unconventional inner lives. Unwilling to indulge in fantasy, we hide out even from ourselves. We end up not only publicly nicer than any authentic person actually is, but too good to be true even within the privacy of our imaginations.

We hide our true selves by choosing ways of living aimed only at lessening the risk of disapproval from those we depend on for protection. Our accommodation may lessen the chances that they will abandon us, but safeguards as stringent as these provide security attained at exorbitant emotional cost. If our caution demands that we continually deceive those whose care we count on, then who will we be to them, and what will they be for us?

Facing fears on our own is risky. But with no one

else to keep us safe from harm, we have to take care of ourselves no matter how afraid we feel. Taking charge of our own safety requires us to accept personal responsibility for distinguishing between feeling afraid when there is no real need and recognizing threat when we face actual danger. If we are willing to risk discerning the difference for ourselves, and to put in perspective how others tell us to see such distinctions, we increase our emotional options and expand our range of personal freedom.

# Feeling Secure Is Not the Same As Being Out of Danger

In medieval times, as a way of instilling the courage needed to deal with danger, a magician named Merlin established a school for aspiring dragon-slayers. One young knight in the class was so frightened that Merlin had to issue the timid student a "magic sword" to help him overcome his terror. Armed with this protective security, the formerly terrified young man completed every assignment with ease and returned triumphantly to class with a rescued maiden at his side and the head of a slain dragon in his hand.

One day, when the young knight had tracked down a particularly ferocious dragon who held a lovely virgin captive, to his dismay he discovered that he had taken the wrong sword from Merlin's supply rack. Undaunted by his terror, he swung the sword and, to his amazement, deftly disposed of the dragon. Returning to class, he reported his bewilderment at having overcome his fear, even though he was not armed with Merlin's special weapon.

Smiling wryly, the master replied, "You mean you *really* believed that there is such a thing as a magic sword? You could have gotten yourself killed."

* * *

How can we tell the difference between simply *feeling* scared and actually being in danger, or between only-*feeling* secure and really being safe? In the family I grew up in, the sole criterion for assessing the safety or danger of an activity was whether or not it made my mother nervous.

My father stated his standard for judging risk repeatedly: "Your mother is a sick and sensitive woman. She only wants the best for you. So before you do anything on your own, just keep in mind that it might upset her. If it is something Mother might worry about, then you'll know that it's dangerous and that you shouldn't be doing it." Apart from that fallible litmus test, I was taught to ignore my own feelings of personal alarm. If my mother felt secure, then it was silly for me to feel scared.

For example, from the time I was a very small child, I loved playing in the ocean. I could have gone on wading and diving under the waves for hours. But after a few minutes in the water, I was always ordered back to the family blanket, not because the water was too cold or too rough, or because the shifting sandbars or strong undertow might threaten my life. The issue was always the same. My mother believed that I was getting "overexcited," or she worried that when I was not at her side with her watching over me, some terrible accident might befall me. The waves made her so nervous that she herself never went into the water.

When I reached adolescence, I was drawn to another territory that my mother fearfully avoided. Hanging around the streets at night seemed safer to me than staying at home with the family, but I had to be home by twelve because my mother knew that "after midnight, terrible things happen to young boys." Without making it clear whether the danger was violence or sex,

14

she insisted that she could not sleep a wink if I was out after the witching hour.

There were periods when my father worked out of town for weeks at a time. When he was on the road, the nocturnal world outside of our apartment seemed even more menacing to my mother. Although break-ins and burglaries were infrequent in our neighborhood in those days, she had fitted the doors with triple bolts and double chains, and installed security locks on our fifth-floor windows. The fire escape window was nailed shut. Had there been a fire, we might have burned to death, but at least we would have been safe from intruders entering our home to rob or rape my mother.

My father's absence increased her anxiety about my staying out late. On weekends, I continued my pursuit of adventure, but, as she put it, "only over my dead body." No matter how late I got home, she was sure to be sitting up, waiting and worrying. Because of her recurrent vision of me "God forbid, laying bleeding to death in some alley," she often called the police to check on my whereabouts.

I found it more and more difficult to trust my own judgment about what was dangerous and what was safe. My father's father drank too much and could not support his family, and my mother's father had deserted my grandmother and their eleven children to run off with another woman. My parents' anxiety about alcohol made me afraid to drink, and their fear of heterosexual promiscuity further increased my shyness with girls.

Like many other parents in those days, they knew nothing about drugs, and so they never warned me about the dangers of doing dope. If they understood anything about homosexuality, it was too unspeakable to mention. As a result, although I avoided alcohol, and dated more awkwardly and infrequently than I might have, I sampled a wide variety of drugs with minimal anxiety, and calmly spent most of one summer hanging around with a bunch of drag queens.

My interest in that homosexual subculture ended as abruptly as it began, but for years I went on smoking marijuana, hashish, and opium, and popping a variety of pills. Only when I saw friends get hooked, sicken, overdose, and die, did I recognize the danger of what I was doing. Occasionally I dealt enough drugs either to offset the cost of my own buys, or to accommodate fellow users. I stopped dealing when I saw friends arrested and jailed. Attempting to sublimate my dangerous desires, I wrote a term paper titled "Marijuana, Weed of Crime." My parents never read the paper, but they were pleased with the good grade I received.

Desperately seeking their protection, I left some joints on top of my dresser. When my parents inquired about the evidence I had planted for them to find, I insisted on making an expurgated confession of my involvement with drugs. Seemingly unperturbed, they assured me that they were certain I wouldn't have anything more to do with narcotics. Because dope was not a source of anxiety for *them*, they denied any danger it might have posed for me.

Instead of learning to look at my own anxieties and to respect them, I was taught to give priority to theirs. It took me a needlessly long time to learn to distinguish real from false alarms, and reliable from unreliable signals of safety. Children whose fears are overshadowed by parental standards of shame and guilt are discouraged from testing out limits for themselves. These inhibitions often leave them unclear about the boundary between safety and danger.

Parents need to warn very young children that some situations that seem safe are really dangerous, and that others can be scary without any threat of actual harm. Beyond giving instructions aimed at protecting the child from innocent misconceptions, parents need to support the child's confidence in listening to his or her own

16

appropriate innate signals of safety and danger. Some instinctual signals of impending threat are identified intuitively by the child (signals such as the biological warning of impending pain evoked by the pressure of a sharply pointed object touching the skin). Other indicators of danger must be taught: for example, the skull-and-crossbones label that identifies poisonous substances. Both the instinctual and the acquired indicators are simple directives that elicit avoidant or protective measures to keep us safe from harm.

*We must learn to tell false alarms from real ones.* This is a necessary (though not a sufficient) distinction for allowing us to decide which risks are worth taking, and which are not.

Sitting in a summer cabin, we may hear the buzzing of insects outside. This noise is a sure signal that if we go out for an evening walk in the woods, there is a high probability we will be bitten by mosquitoes. Even so, rather than choose to stay stuck indoors, we might well accept the trivial risk of getting stung in order to enjoy the pleasure of that romantic adventure.

When prospective danger is too catastrophic to be worth the risk (as in the case of a surprise nuclear attack), even false alarms are warnings worth tolerating. It is not enough to remain alert to our inner warnings of alarm; we must also assess risk in terms of our personal values. Originally, signals of fear are established to announce only credible probability of real and present danger. But the greater the risk to whatever we value most, the more reason we may have to respond to *any* signals of alarm, even if occasionally they turn out to be false. Our willingness to act on false alarms in facing the terrifying threat of total annihilation does *not* necessarily imply that we are fearfully overreacting.

A recent federal government study commissioned by the U.S. Department of Energy shows how situations of low-risk/real-alarm may be confused with those of high-risk/false-alarm.[1] In this study of the psychology of phobic fear of nuclear energy, the public's fear of nuclear power is likened to a neurotic fear of flying based on an inflated expectation that the plane may crash. The director of the study, a psychiatrist who is president of the Phobia Society of America, insists that both fears are psychopathologically disproportionate to the actual risks involved. Consequently, he believes that the public's antinuclear reaction amounts to "phobic thinking."

Rather than consider this concern about the possibility of a catastrophic accident as reasonable alarm calling for practical protection, the study categorizes it as a symptom to be cured. Comparable arguments were leveled at reactions to the Three Mile Island's power plant coming within half an hour of meltdown. Despite the more recent tragedy at Chernobyl, denials of danger continue to come from some quarters. Under conditions so awesomely threatening, at times it's better to over-react than to risk annihilation.

We want to live our lives reasonably safe from harm, but we don't want to spend them hiding under the covers because we are afraid of the dark. How are we to distinguish situations in which it's appropriate to be scared from those in which we can safely remain at ease?

First, we must make certain that when we avoid risk, we do so out of our *own* fear of what might harm us, rather than out of anxiety that our actions will make other people uneasy, or make them think that we are weak or foolish. Next, we must evaluate for ourselves, whether our fear of real or imagined danger justifies what we must do to manage. Finally, in threatening situations, we must each take responsibility for deciding for ourselves whether the rewards of taking or avoiding a particular action are worth the risk.

If we are unduly influenced by how other people may judge what we do with our options (whether in the direction of cautious avoidance, or of bold action), we are likely to live lives not wholly our own. Some of us characteristically operate with reckless abandon; some of us constrict our curiosity with chronic caution.

In either case, *unless we learn to recognize risk in personal terms*, we sacrifice the option of doing as we please. Unless we are willing to act on our own and to decide for ourselves, we end up settling for narrow negotiation between the empty awards of others' approval and the deceptive deadliness of their disapproval. Security that depends on what we imagine other people will think of us may seem safer than taking our chances, but calling the shots as we see them can be a hell of a lot more exciting.

# Fascination with Fear

Ghost stories and tales of the supernatural have always been popular. Throughout history, storytellers, balladeers, and writers have enthralled audiences with accounts of uncanny events that both stimulated and satisfied humankind's fascination with fear.

Among some of the earliest horror fiction still available are ancient Sanskrit stories of a Hindu king whose struggles with the fearful darkness have been recorded in the twenty-five tales of *The King and the Corpse*.[1] His story begins at a time when the secretly fearful king has concealed his anxieties under an impenetrable cover of imperial complacency.

Disguised as a holy beggar, an evil sorcerer ensnares the king by inviting his help in a rite of exorcism. The king agrees to meet with the sorcerer on the night of the next new moon at the funeral ground that serves as a crematorium for the dead and a hanging place of criminals.

The blindness and complacency of the secretly fearful royal character are to be exposed on this dark burial ground that is a dark mirror of his own secret self. The beggar turns out to be not only a sanctimonious ascetic, but a mad magician as well. The king finds himself faced with the ghosts of his own fear-filled past. This ordeal allows him to attain a life of uncertain hopes balanced by risk-filled spontaneity.

In the darkness of the appointed night, armed with sword and cloaked to disguise his royal identity, the king approaches the terrible rendezvous at the burial ground. Charred skulls and skeletons lay scattered about. Ghouls and demons fill the air with a hideous uproar. The old sorcerer draws a magic circle on the ground. He instructs the king to go to the other end of the burning ground where there is a great tree from which a hanged man dangles. The king is to cut down the corpse and carry it back to the magic circle.

With trembling determination, the king approaches the hanging tree whose strange fruit he is to pluck. He climbs the tree and cuts the rope with his sword. As the body falls, he hears it moan. He examines the rigid figure to see if it is still alive. A ghostly laugh breaks from its throat. The king challenges the ghost, but the moment he speaks, the corpse flies back to the tree branch.

When the king climbs up to cut it it down again, he makes sure he utters no sound. Hoisting the body onto his shoulder, he begins to trudge back across the burial ground. Before he has taken many steps, the corpse speaks into his ear, saying "let me tell you a tale to ease your task."

The king does not reply. The ghost goes on to tell its tale. When the telling is done, the ghost poses a question about the story's meaning, warning the king, *"If you know the answer but do not reply, your head will burst into a hundred pieces."*

Believing he knows the answer, the king dares not remain silent. But as he finishes his reply to the ghost's question, the corpse lets out a groan of mock agony, flees from the king's shoulder, and returns to hang once more from the tree limb. Wearily the king goes back, cuts down the corpse once more, and again begins his burdensome trek.

Again and again the macabre scene is repeated. Each time, the ghost torments the king with a new riddling tale, and the threat that the king's head will explode if he knows the answer but does not reply. Again and again, the king becomes aware of answers that he wishes he did not know. Maddeningly, every insight he offers earns him only another tiring trip back to the hanging tree to which the corpse has mockingly returned.

There are twenty-four tales in all, but only twenty-three trudging returns to the tree. The king can find no answer to the twenty-fourth riddle. Acknowledging to himself at last that some questions cannot be answered, the king is finally able to deliver the corpse to the magic circle.

Satisfied at last, the ghost takes leave of the corpse. As the specter emerges, it warns the king:

Listen to what I have to tell you, and, if you value your own good, do exactly as I say. That beggar monk is a very dangerous imposter. With his powerful spells he is going to force me to reenter this corpse, which he will then use as an idol. What he plans to do is to place it in the center of his magic circle, worship me there as a divinity, and, in the course of the worship, offer you up as the victim. You will be ordered to fall down and do me reverence, first on your knees, then prostrate, in the most slavish attitude of devotion, with your head, hands, and shoulders touching the ground. He will then attempt to decapitate you with a single stroke of your own sword.

There is only one way to escape. When you are ordered to go down, you must say: Please demonstrate this slavish form of prostration, so that I, a king unused to such attitudes, may see how one assumes such a posture of worship. And when he is lying flat on the ground, strike off his head with a quick cut of the sword. In that instant, all the supernatural power that this sorcerer is trying to conjure from the sphere of the celestials will fall to you. And you will be a potent king indeed![2]

By the time the king reaches the magic circle, the magician is ready to make use of the fruits of the king's ghoulish task. The sorcerer takes the body and sets it in the middle of the circle which is by then beset with ground bones lit with burning wicks of corpse fat. He adorns it, chants incantations that compel the ghost to reenter the body, and begins to worship it just as the specter predicted.

Forewarned, the king does not comply with the command to prostrate himself in this black mass. Instead, he uses the suggested ruse, and as the sorcerer demonstrates the worshipful pose, the king slashes off his head and cuts out his heart.

When he presents these bloody offerings to the specter, a howl of jubilation arises from the other spirits of the burial ground. They too have been rescued from the terrifying thrall of enchantment attempted by the necromancer.

Gratefully acknowledging the king's triumph over the evil sorcerer, the ghost offers to grant any wish he chooses. Wisely, the king asks only that the tale of this terrible night be retold all over the world and throughout the ages. The specter promises that it will be so, and so it has been.

Scary stories sometimes serve as safe access to our darkest and most personal fearful fantasies, but we cannot expect just any piece of horror fiction or tale of terror to turn up to be an enlightening experience. At best, most spooky stories offer only entertainment. The worst ones simply expose us to sensational shock, use-

23

less upset, and lingering flashbacks of unrewarding edginess. Only in the last hundred years has there emerged a genre of spooky stories sufficiently informed by depth psychology to facilitate such self-awareness in its readers.

Before discussing the sort of scary stories that can encourage personal growth and release us from needless fear, we need to pause long enough to examine the apparent paradox of our occasional fascination with fear. Why do we sometimes willingly expose ourselves to frightening experiences we could otherwise avoid?

It's easy to understand our automatic avoidance of anything that frightens us. But what are we to make of those times when we willingly peer into the shadows of seemingly ominous experiences? Rather than tempt those terrors, it would seem only natural to turn away from whatever is threatening and toward well-lighted, more familiar paths.

At least that is what we usually do. The pedestrian practicality of conventional wisdom lets us make occasional exceptions. For example if a chosen course is not working well, it may make sense to risk unfamiliar alternatives. But whether in the external world or our worlds within, pursuit of the unknown is seen as sensible only when there is outside pressure or an inner longing for improvement.

The proverbial admonitions include: "Don't worry!," "Figure out the right way of doing things and stick with it!" and "If it's not broken, don't fix it!" Depth psychology insists that the soul does not see things that simply. A Hasidic rabbi was once asked, "If we want people to look in, why do we have curtains, and if we do not want them to look in, why have a window at all?" Rabbi Eleazar answered, "When you want someone you love to look in, you draw aside the curtain." To paraphrase his reply in the context of fascination with fear, "When whatever we are afraid of is intriguing enough, we stop hiding under the covers."

When we approach experiences for which we are unprepared we feel apprehension about awkwardness, failure, and ridicule. Even so, to live with liveliness and humor, we must be willing to tolerate the holy insecurity of uncertain outcomes that accompany taking chances. Fortunately, there is often another side to our expectations about the unknown. Along with our apprehensions, we may also feel excited about making new discoveries, mastering untried skills, and trying out unusual experiences.

Like Sir Edmund Hillary, we may climb our Mt. Everests *because they are there*. Or instead, we may act as sensibly as President Kennedy's press secretary, Pierre Salinger. After he had reluctantly accompanied the presidential family in white-water rafting the Colorado River, rather than risk the climb out of the Grand Canyon with the rest of the adventurers, Salinger chose instead to be flown out by helicopter. When asked why he made the ascent by helicopter, he replied, "Because *it* was there."

We can play it safe, or we can take our chances. Our apprehensions about the dangers of harm lurking in the shadows of everything unknown around us is the terror of being destroyed. These terrors go hand in hand with a pervasive anxiety about the unexplored aspects of our inner selves. We fear our darker side may turn out to be so awful that exposing it will result in the horror of separation from the people we depend on for protection.

The silence within us emits almost inaudible whispers of urges we wish we had not heard. Rather than risk learning more about who we are whenever possible, we ignore the threats posed by our "crazy" thoughts and primitive emotions. Instead we choose to imagine ourselves in more comfortably familiar terms. These more conventional self-images seem more acceptable only because we imagine that they elicit the approval of others. For example, we may be tempted to ignore how many buried resentments we have for fear we will discover a dangerously destructive accumulation of unexpressed rage toward those we cling to for security. The unspeakable danger in a child's hatred of his mother is not that he will hurt her. The threat is that if she finds out he hates her, she may abandon him.

We are tempted to banish these unspeakable sounds to the silence within our secret selves, hoping they will go unheard. Such denials make as much sense as ignoring, as if unseen, any intimidating unknown areas in the outer darkness of the world around us. Just as feeling afraid of the dark limits us in adventuring toward opportunities to live out all that we might do in the world, fear of the sounds in the silence within us keeps us from discovering all that we might yet be.

Unexplored inner experiences and all that is unknown outside ourselves often appear ominous. Avoiding the dark mysteries of the soul often seems like simple straightforward good sense. What then are we to make of those times when, without obvious practical reasons for taking the risk, we sometimes undertake adventures that we know will frighten us?

Why do we risk excursions into the dangerous territory of exposure to uncanny experiences? And why do we ride roller-coasters or climb cliffs? What possesses us to consult a psychic or attend a seance? Why read books or watch films advertised as guaranteed to teach us things about ourselves that we are afraid to find out?

We expose ourselves to avoidable frightening experiences for several different reasons. Sometimes we want to enliven an otherwise humdrum, familiar and routine, safe style of living. We gamble, skydive, or pay to enter spooky carnival funhouses in search of instant escape from predictably dull everyday existence.

We take unnecessary risks not only to experience the thrill of simulated danger, but also for the relief of releasing unexpressed tensions. Although we feel fear on a roller-coaster ride, we know that we are really safe. When we rocket down from the heights screaming, "We're going to crash!" our anxiety shifts away from catastrophes we cannot control. All the while we're screaming for our lives, we understand that we'll soon be walking the fairgrounds eating cotton candy.

We can also use our fascination with fear to learn to cope with both the conscious fears that infest our fantasies, and with the unconscious ones that only make themselves known in our nightmares. The first step toward easing the unwanted impact of personal anxieties on our lives is to recognize them and look them straight in the eye. One way we can start to do this is through reading horror fiction and living through the tales of terror found in some popular films and books.

These Gothic pieces allow our imagination safe access to the threatening themes that we must eventually face as fears within our own personalities. Macabre stories offer an easy introduction to eventual confrontation with our more personal anxieties.

We don't need to risk ourselves too much or too soon. There is no shame in doing things the easy way. Why begin by focusing directly on our worst personal fantasies when less dangerous paths are open to us? We can set out in the company of the teller or the central character of a scary story. Territories too frightening to enter unprepared and alone have been mapped for us, and we can explore vicariously the regions that reflect our own as yet uncharted inner fears.

Fascination with fear is an indication that we are ignoring whatever frightens us enough to warrant this attention. Running away may relieve our anxieties momentarily, but lasting ease requires our turning toward what we dread most. In dealing with fear, *the way out is in*.

Two

# Horror Fiction and
# Tales of Terror

# 4

# Scary Stories Offer Access to Personal Fears

None of us is comfortable facing how helpless we feel in the face of unavoidable danger. No one wants to think about the fact that there will be dreaded times when we will fail, lose loved ones, suffer injury and illness, age, wither, and eventually, die.

The Compassionate Buddha instructs us about the ways in which awareness of this universality can ease anxiety, ameliorate suffering, and diminish the grief of making too much of our own situations. In the Parable of the Mustard Seed, a young woman whose little son had died felt grief so great that she could not accept the boy's death.[1] Carrying her dead child on her hip, she took the streets. Going from house to house, she desperately demanded medicine for her son. People saw that she was mad, mocked her, and told her that there was no medicine for the dead.

A sympathetic wise man directed her to the monastery where the Buddha taught. She hurried to the Teacher, and eagerly asked asked for medicine for her son. Smiling serenely, the Buddha answered, "It was wise of you to have come here. This is what you must do. Go to each house in the city, one by one, and fetch tiny grains of mustard seed. But not just any house will do. You must only take mustard seeds from those houses in which no one has ever died."

The mother agreed at once, and set out enthusiastically on her mission. At the first house she knocked at the door saying, "I have been sent by the Exalted One. You are to give me tiny grains of mustard seed. This is the medicine I must have for my son."

When the mustard seed was brought to her, she added, "Before I take the seed, tell me, is this a house in which no one has died?" "Oh no," the householder answered, "the dead from this house are beyond counting." "Then I must go elsewhere," said the mother "The Exalted One was very clear about this. I am to seek out mustard seeds only from those houses that death has not visited,"

On and on she went, from one house to the next. The answer was always the same. In the entire city, there was no house untouched by death. Finally she understood why she had been sent on this hopeless mission. Overcome with feelings, she left the city and carried her dead son to the burning grounds. There she gave him up.

When she returned to the monastery, the softly smiling Buddha asked her, "Did you fetch the tiny grains of mustard seed from the houses without death, as I told you to do?"

The young woman answered, "There are no houses where death is not known. All of humankind is touched by death. My own dear son is dead. I see now that whoever is born must die. Everything passes away. There is no medicine for this but acceptance of it. There is no cure except the knowing. I have faced my fears and found that they are the same as everyone else's. My search for the mustard seeds is over. O Possessor of the Ten Forces, you have given me refuge. Thank you, my Exalted One."

* * *

We won't accept willingly the terror of our inevitable annihilation, nor do we easily acknowledge the horror of having wishes so disgustingly perverse or appallingly destructive that we can hardly stand seeing them in ourselves—much less, expose them to the eyes of others.

Through horror fiction, tales of terror, and other uncanny "entertainments," however, we can face the fears that we are ordinarily inclined to ignore. The grim reaping of these rewards does not require us to believe in ghosts, monsters, or the devil. We merely need to take these ominous images in books and films as metaphors, and allow them to illuminate the personal fears we must face and the anxieties we wish to ameliorate.

A story of the supernatural may alleviate boredom, release tensions, or give us a sense of feeling less helpless in the face of unpredictable dangers. But just because a story is scary does not mean that it can increase our insight into why we sometimes feel afraid when there is no danger. That alone will not foster the personal growth that can free us from some of our irrational fears.

Ancient myths and folktales reflect human frailty—that we are not all that we wish to be, that we lead tentative lives. Myths invoke gods as protectors and demons as sources of danger to soften the terror of unknown aspects of life out of control, and make it more manageable. In folktales others act out the urges we may secretly experience as too awful to claim as our own. When we know others have such urges, we feel comforted.

For a while, the listener or reader can set self aside while wandering in worlds that need never be experienced firsthand. Hearing or reading about demons defeated, ghosts laid to rest, and monsters met and slain reassures us that good triumphs over evil, and that at

33

the story's end, we can return to a world as safe as we could wish it to be.

On the other hand, Gothic writings entrance readers hypnotically with descriptions of believably real characters subjected to nightmarish supernatural events. In haunted medieval castles, housing subterranean vaults laced with secret passages and trap doors, heroic quests are undertaken to rescue maidens from the menace of monsters, ghosts, and demons.

When a Victorian preoccupation with morality elaborated this Gothic literary tradition, a heightened concern with good and evil was added to the fascination with fear. Three prototypes were popular: Mary Shelley's *Frankenstein*,[2] Bram Stoker's *Dracula*,[3] and Robert Louis Stevenson's *Dr. Jekyll and Mr. Hyde*.[4] Although modern day filmmakers have revised these writings, we watch these movies as enthralled as the readers who made them popular in the nineteenth century.

Like our own irrationally frightening personal fantasies, these creatively macabre writings originated in each author's fear-filled inner conflicts. It is astonishing that the powerful allegory *Frankenstein* could have been written by a nineteenth century woman barely nineteen years old. Paradoxically, the story originated out of what might have been the maddest of all English tea parties.

In 1816, on summer holiday on the shores of Lake Geneva, confined to quarters by two weeks of torrential rainstorms, Mary and her poet husband Percy Bysshe Shelley, Lord Byron, and Dr. John Polidori had become a bored band of vacationers. They passed the time by reading aloud to one another from *Fantasmagoria*, a book of German ghost stories. They spooked themselves so successfully that, possessed by the passion of the moment, Percy Shelley ran from the room in horror obsessed with the image of a woman from whose breasts eyes protruded in place of nipples. Fascinated with maintaining the exquisitely fear-filled atmosphere in which they had become immersed, the group agreed that each member would write his or her own ghost story.

Although Mary Shelly had the most trouble getting started, hers was the only story of the four to endure on its own.[5] Doubly intimidated by inexperience and awesomely artistic companions, for several days she modestly maintained that she could not possibly think of a story that could rival theirs.

She describes how she dreamt in the solitude of the night what she could not create in the competition of the day:

I saw the pale student of unhallowed arts kneeling beside the thing he'd put together. I saw the hideous phantasm of a man stretched out, and then, on the working of some powerful engine, show signs of life and stir with an uneasy, half-vital motion. Frightful must it be, for supremely frightful would be the effect of any human endeavor to mark the stupendous mechanism of the Creator of the world. His success would terrify the artist; he would rush away from his odious handiwork, horror stricken. He would hope that, left to itself the slight spark of life which he had communicated would fade, that this thing which had received such imperfect animation would subside into dead matter, and he might sleep in the belief that the silence of the grave would quench forever the transient existence of the hideous corpse which he had looked upon as the cradle of life. He sleeps; but he is awakened; he opens his eyes; behold, the horrid thing stands at his bedside, opening his curtains, and looking on him with yellow, watery, but speculative eyes.[6]

With her husband's encouragement, Mary Shelley completed her nightmare and eventually expanded the short story into the novel known as *Frankenstein*. Contemporary film versions have deleted or condensed the allegorical anxiety of the original in which the monster's unbearable loneliness for a mate drives it to vengeful destructiveness.

The author was willing to face her own fear of the separation that might come from openly competing with men. It took courage for her to complete her nightmare. Sometimes courage can transform our own feared catastrophes into opportunities.[7]

Like the mad scientist in Ms. Shelley's story, Stevenson's protagonist in *Dr. Jekyll and Mr. Hyde* is also interested in exploring forbidden ground. The story also reflects its author's inner fear-filled conflict between obligations to self and society.

Desperately in need of money, Stevenson first wrote his Gothic classic in a three-day potboiling frenzy. Intended as a moneymaking thriller, this shocking piece of horror fiction proved appallingly offensive to his traditionally Victorian wife. After seeing how it upset her, he burned his first draft in the fireplace, and rewrote the socially redeemed version with the morally uplifting elaborations.

Stevenson's nineteenth century horror fiction classic arouses anxiety that stalks the reader's soul from within. In contrast, Stoker's *Dracula* is a tale of terror that evokes intense apprehension of an external evil so impersonal that looking out into the dark unknown chills our souls. The title character is a vampire whose continued existence as one of the living dead hinges on ghoulish, seductive control over those people on whose lifeblood he depends.

Bram Stoker's sickly childhood made for an extended infantile dependence on his morbid mother. He was disabled from infancy on, and so often at the edge of death that, until the age of seven, he could not stand upright. Throughout this early invalidism, Bram's mother entertained him with ghoulish folktales of wailing banshees and with autobiographical accounts of growing up in Ireland during a cholera epidemic that annihilated thousands.

While writing their stories, all three of these classic Gothic authors were haunted by some irrational personal anxiety. Perhaps in part, these personal fears compelled them to tell their tales. When asked why he wrote such scary stories, their contemporary literary heir Stephen King replied: "What makes you think I have a choice?" (Like these other authors, I see the present work as a book I had to write.)

We each have our own demons to fear. I like the Gothic tales because I believe that it is better to live a life filled with colorful contradictions than to wander through a world void of intriguing eccentricities. Standing on my own, naked and afraid, means more to me than safely hiding under the covers where I might miss out on life's wonders.

If outrageous imagination is the wine of madness, then come fill my cup. I'd rather peer into the shadows in the darkness around me, and listen to whispers from the silence within, than play it safe by ignoring all that those shadows and whispers have to offer to make my life more colorful.

This need to face fear is one reason why I became a depth psychotherapist. Another reason is compassion for others coupled with a desire to free them from needless suffering. A fringe benefit is that in therapy they can then join me in the free play of our imaginations.

The contemporary Gothic tales that I will explore as avenues of easing our anxieties are strongly influenced by depth psychology. The first two stories (and the clinical and autobiographical vignettes that accompany

37

them) illustrate the difference between what adults experience as horror, as terror, and as a combination of both. The tales that follow explore some of the ways we cope with deep irrational fear. Some ways work well. Others only make matters worse, particularly in their limiting of our capacity for caring and closeness to other people.

The outlook of depth psychology holds that what we fear enough to make us needlessly unhappy comes from unconscious anxieties and the ways we learned to cope with them in unfortunate early childhood experiences. Talking out our dreams and fantasies enables us to recover lost memories and reshape our personalities. Facing what we fear keeps us safer from neurotic harm.

Because of the increased trust that emerges out of these transformations, we can take better care of ourselves and feel more compassion for others. Without trust, we cannot accept the intimacy of gently holding their trembling hearts in our own extended hands, or of placing ours in theirs.

# 5

# In Some Horror Stories, We Cannot Escape Ourselves

When we read the earliest horror stories, we may feel fear for the safety of the characters, but we feel no danger to ourselves. Reading how the misguided curiosity of mad scientists such as Drs. Frankenstein and Jekyll led them to arrogantly overstep the limits of decency, it becomes apparent that these characters have only themselves to blame. No matter how tantalized by the terror of the tale, as readers we remain safely separated from any feeling of responsibility for the monsters that they unleash and later hunt down to destroy.

Not until American Gothic short stories were influenced by depth psychology did modern horror fiction make readers inescapably aware of their own anxieties. As the insights of depth psychology became integrated into American writing, the more imaginative authors evoked our anxiety less by using stock props and spooky settings than by causing us to identify with the tale's frightened narrator. Unsuspectingly, we are caught up in experiencing his growing personal fears as our own.

Edgar Allan Poe was the first American Gothic short story writer to succeed in seducing readers into sharing the shocking subjective experiences endured by the first-person narrators of his chilling tales.[1] The fear we feel in reading his work is no longer sympathetic concern for unfamiliar characters who encounter unknown dangers. We experience the horror as arising from a source within ourselves. As we understand the ways in which his characters ignore their unacceptably perverse erotic and brutal impulses, we are trapped into awareness of our own unspeakable urges.

In his "Fall of the House of Usher" for example, Poe draws us deeper and deeper into identifying with his narrator.[2] Uncertain as to how we got there, we find that we have crossed over the protective barrier of our usual daylight denials and into nightmarish exposure to all we wish we did not know about ourselves.

The story starts with an unnamed narrator off on a mission of mercy. On a dull soundless autumn afternoon darkly overhung with threatening storm clouds, this seemingly reasonable, decent man rides alone through a dreary countryside. He is responding to an urgent request from Roderick Usher, a boyhood chum he has not seen in many years. Usher's demanding letter was filled with nervous agitation about acute physical illness and mental disorder, entreating his only friend to come help him.

As evening approaches, the narrator comes to the brink of a murky mountain pool, its black surface reflecting the decaying House of Usher that stands at its edge. The empty windows of the grim old house stare out from decaying vegetation that covers and surrounds it, creating an atmosphere of sluggishness, aging discoloration, rot and neglect. He experiences the crumbling condition of the mansion as an omen of unavoidable catastrophe. A barely perceptible crack extending from the roof to the foundation heightens his uneasy impression of instability and imminent collapse.

Crossing the pool on a causeway, he enters the house. The interior is as somber, deteriorated, and phantasmagoric as its facade. The master's studio is dimly lighted by the windows that in his approach had looked like Usher's own empty eyes. They are so long, narrow, and high up that their light is almost inaccessible. Admitting only feeble gleams, the windows obscure the rest of the room in remote shadows, shrouding it in disquieting darkness. The old comfortless and tattered setting evokes within the narrator a sickening atmosphere of sorrow, and a chilling air of stern, deep, and irredeemable gloom.

Out of the shadows in which he reclines on a once-elegant sofa, Usher arises to greet him with cordiality so extravagant that it seems forced. Usher's altered appearance makes it difficult for the narrator to feel in touch with his boyhood companion. The lovely child he once cherished now has the sallow complexion of a cadaver, luminously liquid eyes, thin pallid lips, and a look that lacks vibrancy. His ghastly pallor and the unheeded growth of his silken hair are like the aging, fungus-covered stonework of the exterior of the house itself.

Usher alternates between incoherence and an unconvincing vivaciousness bent on feebly futile attempts to make personal contact. The weighty, slow, and hollow sound of his speech makes him seem almost intoxicated. He describes his illness as an inherited family evil, a nervous affliction without hope of remedy. The morbid acuteness of his senses has left him hypersensitive to any but the blandest of foods, odors, sights, sounds, and touches. Anything stronger inspires him with horror.

In this panicky state, it is not so much any particular or actual danger that he dreads. His grim anxiety is the terror that he might fully feel his fear. Trapped by superstitious belief in the possessive power of the house out of which he has not ventured for many years, Usher has come to believe that its shadowy force peculiarly influences his every experience.

Its gray walls now physically define the personal boundaries of the subjective quality of his existence. At the same time, he attributes the physical and psychological discomforts he suffers to his reaction to the severe chronic illness of his last living relative, his twin sister Madeline, his only companion for many years. Her death would leave him isolated as the last of the Ushers.

At this point, silent as a ghost, Madeline passes through a remote area of the studio and disappears without reacting to their presence. The narrator feels filled with astonishment, dread, and oppressive stupor. On the other hand, acting as if he had not noticed Madeline's soundless coming and going, Usher goes on to describe her disease as an inadequately understood state of apathy and gradual wasting away. That night, she dies.

For several days, neither man speaks of the sister's death, and the narrator tries to console his mourning friend. They busy themselves with poetry, music, and painting, but the host's uneven concentration reveals much of the melancholy that it is intended to obscure. Intermittently he speaks of an obsession with the "sentience of all vegetable things." For the narrator, this semidelusional idea mirrors the atmosphere created by the fungus spread over both Usher's house and his soul, unalterably influencing the family destiny and transforming him into what he has become.

Before burying Madeline, Usher wants to preserve her body in a vault within the house, rationalizing that the family physician is curious about her peculiar disease. The narrator agrees to aid Usher in temporarily entombing the coffin in a small dark damp space below his own guest bedroom. Once used to store dangerous chemicals, the temporary tomb is a secret room, sheathed in copper and protected by a massive iron door. Before bolting the vault, together they unscrew the coffin lid. Madeline's disease has left the mockery of a faint blush on her face, and a leering smile on her lips. The narrator is deeply disturbed by the striking similarity of the faces of the dead sister and the live brother, reflecting an incomprehensible bond of twinship that persists even after death.

After some days of bitter grief, Usher seems more and more mentally disordered. As he roams aimlessly about the house, his pallor grows even more ghastly, and the last light in his eyes seems to fade. His voice trembles in terror as though his agitated mind is belabored by some secret so oppressive that he lacks the courage to express it. Increasingly lost in the vagaries of madness, for hours on end he stares vacantly into space as if listening to some sound imagined in the silence.

The narrator cannot help being affected by his old friend's deteriorating condition, and more and more, Usher's anxiety begins to belong to him as well. Nothing he can do changes his mood. After several days, he can no longer escape his own unbearable edginess.

Unable to sleep, he peers into the darkness. He hears low, indefinite sounds that overpower him with horror so unaccountable and unendurable that he gets up and paces back and forth across his bedroom. Soon he makes out a light footstep on an adjoining staircase. Usher enters the bedroom with a look of mad hilarity on his face, asking the narrator if he has seen "it" too. Shading his lamp, the host opens one of the windows to the storm outside. The intensity of the wind shifts the low-hanging dense clouds till they seem to be careening against the night sky. The entire scene glows in an unnatural light that surrounds the mansion.

The narrator tries to distract Usher from his fascination with the horror that holds him by explaining it all away as electrical phenomena of the storm. In an attempt to reassure them both, he reads aloud to his host, but is not able to alleviate his agitation. The tale tells of a romance in which a hermit beats down the planks of a door. Indistinct echoes of such sounds come from some remote portion of the house. Gradually, the noises described in the story he is reading are more and more clearly echoed in the building about them. He is uncertain whether Usher has heard the sounds as well. His host's demeanor changes, his lips tremble as if murmuring inaudibly; his head drops to his chest, and his entire body rocks from side to side as if he has become lost within himself.

The narrator continues reading the story aloud. As the knight in the tale slays a dragon that falls with a "mighty great and terrible ringing sound," a similar clamor in the house brings the narrator to his feet. Usher remains stonily rigid, displaying a strong shudder and a sickly smile, and murmuring gibberish.

He then tells the narrator that he has heard it too, that he has been hearing it for a long, long time, but till now has not dared to speak of it. What he hears are his sister's first feeble movements in the hollow coffin. His horror is that she is coming to upbraid him for his haste that has entombed her alive. He goes on to explain to his guest that the sound they hear is the horrible beating of her heart, and that she is now standing just beyond the bedroom door.

As he speaks, the wind blows the door open. Outside stands the enshrouded figure of Madeline with blood on her white robes and evidence of struggle in her emaciated frame. For a moment, she trembles on the threshold, and then reels across, falling heavily into the room and onto her brother. By the time they hit the floor, both are dead, victims of the horrors Usher had anticipated.

The story ends with the narrator fleeing from the

room and out of the house. As he crosses the old causeway in the storm, turning in response to a wild light, he sees the once barely discernible fissure rapidly widen until the mighty walls break apart and the mansion collapses. As the House of Usher falls into the deep, dank mountain pool, sullenly and silently the dark waters close over it.

As we read the story, our own uneasiness keeps pace with the narrator's growing awareness of his anxiety. Along with him, at first we rationalize our discomfort as no more than an unwarranted reaction to the natural sounds of creaking boards and stormy winds. But as his self-protective skepticism begins to crumble in response to the insidious impact of Usher's mad imaginings, our own comforting common sense approach also starts to erode.

As we become aware of anxiety that can no longer be explained away, we begin to feel more and more afraid. Like the teller of the tale, we cannot continue to believe that our dread is caused by innocuous external events that are not really worth worrying about. We are no longer able to shake off the increasingly irrational fear that arises from some secret source of horror within ourselves.

Bit by bit, we are induced to experience the eerie and inescapable isolation of feeling ourselves alone and unprotected in a strange place. Along with the narrator, we are seemingly innocent bystanders caught up in a situation beyond control or comprehension. Our sensibility is so stunned that our mind has lost its way.

Along with these feelings of horror comes our understanding that, like Usher, at times we too are unacceptably perverse. We have all had our own evil urges, and on occasion have acted out some of our awful impulses. At the very least, we have all lied, acted unfairly, and bounded our ethics with rubber fences.

When we are frightened and intensely aware of the horror from within, we are most susceptible to imagining that if something bad is about to happen, then we ourselves are somehow to blame. At such times, it is easy to imagine that we are unworthy of the comfort and protection we want. We make unspoken entreaties to God or to the Fates, swearing that if only this situation ends safely, we will never again think about our awful impulses, let alone act on them.

We have all known times when the boundaries between self and others were obscured, and our sense of separateness dissolved. Like most primitive experiences, these can break either way. On one side is the ecstasy of union with the beloved. On the other is the overwhelming experience of our immersion in anxiety.

For example, a close friend worries that some seemingly innocuous physical symptom means that he or she is going to die, or that under stress he will fall apart and do something crazy. We start out trying to reassure him that everything is all right, but then we realize that we're glad it's happening to him or her instead of to us. Sometimes our own uneasiness gets out of hand. As we become aware of how anxious we begin to feel, our own fear expands to the point where we ourselves are engulfed with horror. It is then that we are tempted to imagine that what we fear has occurred because of how awful we are within our secret selves.

I see now that this was the case in my early unconscious motivation for becoming a psychotherapist. Unwittingly I transformed my infantile wish to kill my mother into an attempt to cure her (and myself) of the anxieties that engulfed our relationship. Had I anticipated the house of horrors into which fascination with my own fears eventually ushered me, I might have hesitated in making that career choice.

Like so many other psychotherapists seeking the seeming security of this curiously sullen craft, I started out innocently unaware of my underlying motivations. The lower-middle-class subculture of New York Jewry I grew up in provided an array of acceptable explanations for choosing this seemingly sensible and rewarding means of making a living.

Justifications for my ambitions included: Personal Ethics (there were in the world few jobs worth doing, and fewer still that I would do well enough to warrant attempting as a life's work); Economics (a professional man is certain to be a good provider); Social Status (all respectable jobs require enough formal education to ensure working indoors without getting your hands dirty); Ethnic Aspirations (Gentiles would always call me "doctor," never "Jew-Bastard" ); and a Good Guy Image (I would appear to be a sane decent savior of crazy, perverse pariahs).

But my more private psychological needs were the determining factor. I was sometimes marginally conscious of some less acceptable aspirations, but for the most part kept them to myself. Included among them were: Mock Heroics (because I myself was so courageous, I would inspire my patients to overcome their pathological fears); Outrageous Infantilism (I would at last succeed in curing my crazy parents, reclaiming the happy childhood I had missed out on, and recover from my own anxieties without ever having to acknowledge how awful I had become convinced I was); and Perverse Prurience (in the guise of the pure healer, I could experience vicariously the patients' wild and impure adventures that I was too timid and self-righteous to pursue on my own).

Like both the narrator and the reader of Poe's short stories, I was innocently unaware of the horrors into which I was heading when I began to work with psychotherapy patients. It took me a while to recognize that it was impossible for me to be truly open to another person's fears without experiencing unexpected anxieties of my own. With patients like George, projective identification is unavoidable.

This young government attorney sought psychotherapy because of chronic complaints of poor job performance and an inability to maintain satisfying relationships with either friends or lovers. Despite his longing for closeness, George complained that his desperate attempts to get along with other people seldom worked out.

When he entered therapy, George was totally unaware of how much other people were put off by his transparently manipulative flattery, offers of unasked-for favors, and demands for appreciative responses to his unconvincing tokens of admiration. His dread of feeling rejected caused him to be careless about his own part in relationships and impatient about attaining immediately reassuring outcomes. Running scared, he pushed for acceptance, unaware of why the people whose approval he pursued so often backed off.

From the moment of our first meeting, George displayed this demanding helplessness, obviously expecting me to make things right. He began the session by silently waiting for me to tell him what to do. When I offered a nonjudgmental observation about this approach, he reacted by whining in a frightened and pathetic way that now I was blaming him for being himself. He pointed out that he had come to me for emotional help because of my "wonderful reputation for being an expert in such matters." He said I knew all about therapy while he was totally ignorant about what he needed to do. He assured me that if only I would do my part by advising him about what was expected, he would gladly do whatever it was I wanted.

At first I felt secure and confident. My initial task was simply to invite his attention to how helpless he felt, and how much he depended on me to know what was best for him. George responded with alarm to my friendly detachment, saying: "You're frightening me! I came to you for therapy because I don't know what to do to get people to like me. You accuse me of being a bad patient. I know that! That's my problem. I never know what to do to please people. If I knew how to solve that problem, I wouldn't need your help. Now even you don't like me. You'll probably throw me out of therapy."

Every observation I made he interpreted as a criticism, but when I pointed that out, his anxious agitation only increased. As his list of accusations of my incompetence grew longer, I began to find the anguished intensity of his voice increasingly unsettling. He went on (and on, and on): "So now I have another problem. I came here for you to help me with my neurosis, and all you do is accuse me of acting neurotic. The way you talk to me makes me even more nervous and insecure than I was before I met you." Whatever else I said (or did not say) seemed to spiral us further and further into the depths of his disappointment about how I misunderstood him and was unwilling to help him, and his increasing fear that he would never learn how to get along with other people.

George made it clear how unfair it was for me to expect too much of him while stubbornly refusing to make him feel better. "I already feel like a jerk!" he complained. "When you point that out, it just makes me more afraid that there's no hope for me. Now even my therapist dislikes me."

Whatever else I said only seemed to increase his anxiety about being unacceptable, leaving him certain that I was no more trustworthy than anyone else in his unhappy life. Not wanting him to feel like a jerk (or me either), I tried not talking. But my silence increased his anguish even more than my words. He was sure that I found him unworthy of my attention. For the moment, he had succeeded in failing once again, and I had ended up feeling like a jerk.

George had been raised to believe it was his fault that his parents found him unsatisfactory. He grew up dreading disappointment, and while openly criticizing himself for causing his own downfall, he secretly blamed others for all his troubles. My attempts to reassure him were as awkward and excruciating as trying to comfort a burn victim, and my attentive silences caused anxiety that again he was being abandoned.

In turn, I began to respond to his hypersensitivity as confirmation that in my clumsiness, I was truly the horror he beheld. I hated him for making me feel that way. Alternately, we experienced each other as the awful child and as the mother who had found us unfit.

All of this took place over a span of several weeks. I began by being interested in getting to know him, feeling challenged by the barriers he set up, and working hard at exploring other avenues that might encourage a therapeutic alliance. Gradually I came to feel helplessly unable to establish a satisfying relationship with him. At times I felt so awful that it seemed arrogant to consider myself a psychotherapist.

In desperation, I searched my soul for the reasons our relationship was not working. Eventually I heard the echoes of horrible childhood reactions to my mother's raging: "You're so insensitive. Everything you try, you do like a clumsy ox, hurting the people who care the most. Only a mother like me would put up with you. After a while, even I won't be able to save you from the punishment you deserve: first reform school, and then, God forbid, life in prison."

Often after an hour with George, I felt as monstrously unfit for human company as I had as a youth. Once more it was clear to me that my mother had been right. Cruelly insensitive and horribly heavy-handed, I would surely drive away even those who were willing to suffer because they loved me.

For a long while I could not listen to his horror stories without hearing interfering echoes of my own. As the last of seven considerably older children, George was supposed to have made his middle-aged parents happy. But instead of bringing golden light to their later years, he was told that he made them so miserable they wished he had never been born.

He could not see that it was in reaction to his aggressively insatiable efforts to get me to take care of him that I withdrew with a sense of my own insufficiency. His indictment of me as uncaring and inept awakened old horrors implanted early by my own mother's projections of anything about herself that she experienced as unacceptable. Repeatedly, George and I burdened each other with the implicit unkept promise: "If only you hid the horror of how awful you are, then I would take care of you, make you feel secure, and keep you safe from harm."

To protect himself, George had learned to target other people's sore spots, and to control them with the tyranny of his own touchiness. When I told him how he made me feel and how vulnerable I was to rejection, he began to understand his impact on me and to feel free to respond more softly. But for a long time, he found it difficult to believe that I was afraid that he would want nothing more to do with me, or that I valued the times when we were able to meet without our usual struggle.

Once he understood that both his positive and his negative emotional impact on me was as much my reaction as his doing, he felt both relieved of blame and safer in taking responsibility for his part. As I was able to separate out my inner horror from his passive assaults, I became able to hear his complaints without feeling upset. He could then risk showing his hidden hatred openly with decreasing fear that it would separate us.

At times, we hold back on expressing our emotions because of someone else's anxiety. When we can admit to ourselves that some aspects of ourselves seem too unlovable to expose, and understand that everyone else has some of the same fears, it becomes possible for us to sort out past fears from present dangers.

Rather than strike back or withdraw, we have the option of telling the other person how we really feel. For example, a happily married young couple has two children. The husband sees his wife's anxious preoccupation with caring for the children as an indication that being with him no longer turns her on. As a way of avoiding this awful feeling he withdraws by immersing himself in watching ballgames on television.

In response the wife may feel that he is rejecting her as unlovable. She then attempts to avoid her own anxiety by attacking him with the accusation, "All you ever want to do is to watch the damned tube." Once she understands the fear she feels and where it comes from, she can approach the situation with more appealing vulnerability, saying something like: "I know that seeing this game is important to you, but I'm feeling sort of scared and lonely. I can wait a while, but I'd really like us to spend some time together soon."

She might then be relieved and surprised to hear her husband respond by saying: "I'd love to. It's not that good a game anyway. And besides I was only watching it because you seemed so busy. When you stay so wrapped up in the children, I end up feeling afraid it's because of something I've done that you feel is too awful to forgive."

Either the wife or the husband could have interceded to break this circle of fear. Unfortunately, in our culture men have not yet learned to be as much at ease as women in making themselves vulnerable.

Facing our fears of whatever within us we imagine is too unacceptable to expose allows us to express our longing for closeness without either belittling ourselves, or blaming the other. Bridging the separation begins by exposing our fears to the other.

# 6

# Some Monsters We Meet Mirror Our Secret Selves

Like ourselves, the world in which we live can be caring and compassionate, or it can be impersonally evil, or anything in the spectrum in between. If we ignore our own monstrous capacities for evil and attempt to sustain a sentimentally sweet and sane vision of the world around us, we increase our susceptibility to the unexpected impact of all that we banish to the unknown. When we try to imagine that we have life under control, we often end up being less in charge of what happens to us.

We encounter this terrifying interplay between insistence on our own innocence and sentimental sugarcoating of life's dangers when we read Flannery O'Connor's chilling tale, "A Good Man Is Hard to Find."[1] It is an alarming account of grotesque agents of uncontrollable evil who kill an innocent family of ordinary southern country folk. The story's chief character is the Grandmother who wants to believe that she and her family are all good people, and consequently no evil should befall them. When she collides with her criminal counterpart, her simple saintliness is no match for its opposite. Known only as The Misfit, this psychopathic killer is more deeply devoted to his active anarchy than she is in her passive acceptance of traditional morality.[2]

These good country people are a family of six who set out on a sightseeing trip from Georgia to Florida. The Grandmother is a self-declared Christian who has carefully dressed for the trip so that in the event of an accident, "anyone seeing her dead on the highway would know at once that the she was a lady." Beneath her apparent piety, she is somewhat mean-spirited and spitefully manipulative.

Unable to talk the others into going to Tennessee, she has settled for getting her own way in minor matters. Despite her son-in-law's objections, she has stealthily stowed away her cat in a basket in the back seat of his car. She has also badgered the others into taking a short side trip to a house only she wants to visit. Having already described the place as more interesting than it actually is, and unwilling to admit that she does not know its exact location, she directs them to a deadly detour. As they drive down this isolated and untraveled road, her cat jumps onto her son-in-law's shoulder and claws him. He swerves the wheel and the car overturns in a gulch.

The Grandmother's manipulations unexpectedly cause them to tumble into an accidental encounter with an unmanageably impersonal menace. The as yet unidentified Misfit and his two henchmen appear on a ridge and are mistaken for saviors come to rescue the family from their automobile accident.

When the three men descend to the ditch, the attitude of the dominant figure is unexpectedly cold and cruelly controlling. He carries a gun. Despite the Grandmother's almost automatic temptation to ignore the frightening familiarity of his face, she impulsively acknowledges recognizing him from photos she saw earlier in a newspaper account of the three convicts' escape from prison.

In an attempt to transform their terrifying situation into a friendly meeting, she begins to cry, imploring The Misfit, "You wouldn't shoot a lady, would you?" He answers, "I would hate to have to." In response, she screams insistently, "I know you're a good man. You don't look a bit like you have common blood. I know you must come from nice people!"

Coolly, The Misfit instructs his accomplices to take the other family members into the adjoining woods, one or two at a time, explaining to the Grandmother that he and his men need to replace their buried prison uniforms.

Trying to turn away her worst fears, and even now insistently sympathetic, she still seeks to reform him. "If you would pray, Jesus would help you," she assures him.

The Misfit agrees, but goes on to state flatly that he is doing all right by himself and does not want any help. He explains to her, "I found out that crime don't matter. You can do one thing or you can do another, kill a man or take a tire off his car, but sooner or later you're going to forget what it is you done and just be punished for it."

Hearing pistol shots and piercing screams echoing out of the woods, the Grandmother becomes increasingly apprehensive. No longer able to deny that her preachings about Jesus have had no effect on the evil attitudes of The Misfit, she is reduced to trying a little tenderness. In desperation, she claims the criminal as her own, murmuring sweetly, "Why you're one of my babies. You're one of my own children!" But when she reaches out to touch his shoulder, he springs back as if bitten by a snake, and shoots her three times through the chest.

When his henchmen return, one of them remarks on

what a good talker she was. The Misfit agrees, "She would of been a good woman, if it had been somebody there to shoot her every minute of her life."

We are all open to uninvited targeting by impersonal evil, not because some deadly danger bears our name, but only because it is addressed: TO WHOM IT MAY CONCERN. Criminals assault innocent victims. Accidental injuries, epidemic diseases, wars, storms, and floods can harm anyone who happens to be in the wrong place at the wrong time. These unexpected hazards can terrorize any of us. We are right to fear these uncontrollable catastrophes. Sensible cautions can help, but none of us can keep ourselves completely safe from harm.

Ignoring the risks of daily living is dangerous. If we imagine ourselves as so especially good that we are less likely than others to be subject to undeserved dangers, unwittingly we become more unprepared to deal with sudden disasters. When we attempt to ease our minds by denying our apprehensions, we are likely to be recklessly faced with risks that we could have avoided.

Part of the problem is that most people are conservative about ensuring their safety. Often we are unwilling to act in the interests of probable prevention or to invest in precautions until the danger is upon us. We are more willing to expend energy and money in burglarproofing our homes *after* a break-in than to set up the safeguards that might have prevented it.

Even after we have been robbed, we may be misled by the "gambler's fallacy" to conclude incorrectly that once a situation has turned out badly, chances are that next time it will turn out well. Uncomfortable with the ambiguity of probabilities, we insist on embracing the security of imagined absolute certainty, especially when we want to have our own way. When a film we very much want to see is playing only at a theater in a neighborhood we know is dangerous, we are more likely to say to ourselves, "I know nothing bad will happen to me tonight" than to say, "I know the risks of getting mugged if I go to that theater, but I want so much to see that film, I'll accept the risk and exercise appropriate caution when I walk those mean streets."

Ironically, our insistence that we can be sure of our safety only increases our susceptibility to harm. Denying dangers we find difficult to identify with, or to comprehend, we are inclined to delegate responsibility for our safety to experts and authorities. We argue that they *must* know what they are doing or they wouldn't have the job of taking care of us.

At times when we cannot be certain about the risks we face, we may deliberately settle for accepting dangers like drinking, smoking, and driving that let us keep the illusion that we are in control. We are willing to accept greater risks in areas that we *imagine* are under our command than we are in those aspects of our lives that seem out of our control. Helpless to do anything effective about the industrial pollution of our external environment, we willingly engage in personally polluting our insides with alcohol, tobacco, preservatives, and drugs.

Paradoxically, the false sense of comfort afforded by this ill-informed feeling of control leaves us less in charge of our lives, and at higher risk of early death. Dangerous overconfidence distracts us from learning what we need to know to best protect ourselves.

For example, consider the fact that although the risks of nuclear power are regarded as "involuntary, uncontrollable, unknown, inequitably distributed, likely to be fatal, [and] potentially catastrophic," automobiles that kill so many more people every day seem safe enough to warrant little worry.[3] A fear-filled life may not be worth living, but a life lived as if there is nothing to fear is not likely to last very long.

We all suffer some exposure to the terror of external and impersonal evil. Some of us encounter its personal equivalent too early in life, and in terms too harsh or excessive. If this happens when children most need the security that comes from dependably accessible parental protection, the results can be disastrous. Their ability to cope with fear and assess risk is diminished, and as adults, they end up facing daily lives almost entirely preoccupied with dealing with the dread of more pervasive imagined dangers than most of us ever meet.

Understanding the experience of people so obsessed with terror can help us to better understand our own apprehensions about the catastrophic threats we may encounter. A psychotherapy patient of mine, whom I will call Cathy, was reared in an environment so emotionally dangerous that her adulthood has been lived in terror despite the absence of actual danger.

The chronically high intensity of her disabling alarm might be expected if Cathy had grown up homeless, unsupported by a family and left to fend for herself in a wartorn culture. Instead (at least in socioeconomic terms), her childhood could be described as stable and secure. She was *not* the product of a broken home. Her parents were law-abiding, materially reliable providers of food, clothing, shelter, and adequate medical care.

Yet from the moment I met her, Cathy seemed easily and inordinately terrified. My office setting, my attitude and appearance, and almost anything I said elicited anguish which she expressed through uncomfortable squirming in her chair, grimacing and flinching as if she expected to be attacked, and uttering intermittent and anguished outcries of "You're frightening me!"

Her presenting problem was emotional upset over the breakup of a relationship. She had left her lover when she learned that although he knew that he had herpes when they met, it was revealed only inadvertently, months after they had begun sleeping together.

Later I learned that she had a history of innocently entering relationships that appeared to offer the acceptance and protection for which she longed, only to back out after being hurt by the betrayal of her trust.

These betrayers included several other therapists, each of whom she had seen for a while before she came to see me. In each instance, Cathy reported that the former therapist had proved untrustworthy and unreliable, and had ended up insisting that she "take care of him!" Therapeutic misalliances were all described as instances in which she felt that her demands had frightened the therapist. One found her "too big a baby," another told her she was "potentially violent," and they all felt that she was "sexually and emotionally too much to handle." She inferred they wanted to be taken care of by her because they seemed to need protection from her volatile emotional outbursts.

At first I was curious about the astonishing contrast between Cathy's primitive and volatile emotional behavior in my office, and the cool streetwise sophistication required in her work with precociously promiscuous, often too early pregnant, and otherwise delinquent ghetto teenagers. Her job also required a competent professional demeanor in dealing with the community agencies whose resources she coordinated to care for these kids who needed so much.

I began to understand Cathy better when she told me that she had been raised as a "service brat." As the youngest of several children of a father who was a committed career military officer, and a mother dedicated to her husband's promotional advances, Cathy's early life had been disrupted again and again each time the family was transferred to a new post.

As a child, she lived in four countries and attended eleven different schools. She had to sacrifice close friends and familiar surroundings to start over as a stranger in a strange land. Her parents urged her to welcome the emotionally educational opportunity afforded by the uprooting, ignoring her grief and anxiety in the interest of instilling a forced "flexibility."

Cathy's father's obsessive preoccupation with his military career, and her mother's social commitments as an "officer's lady" often took priority over their concern for her well-being. They turned over her care to enlisted men who could be summoned to the house for extra duty. Several of these men sexually molested Cathy. When she tried to tell her busy parents about these upsetting episodes, her "tales" were discounted as imagined accounts made up to demand attention.

Too absorbed in their own lives to allow Cathy a self of her own in need of their protection, her parents attributed her fears to a child's wild imaginings. Gradually Cathy gave up pursuing her parents' protection. In its place, she settled for whatever confusing satisfaction she could get from these scary intrusive sexual experiences.

These molesting men provided a perverse substitute for some of the personal attention she found otherwise unavailable. Cathy took care of their needs without upsetting her parents with her own. This came about at an exorbitant psychological cost to her. She blamed herself both for being an emotional bother to her parents, and for being an evil influence on the men who molested her.

Cathy withdrew further and further into the isolation of an imaginary world of her own. She was able to feel safe and secure only in the care of a strong, reliable imaginary companion she had created in fantasy. After a time even the demands of this guardian angel got out of hand. By the time Cathy came to me for help, she often felt intimidated by "Her" laughing at the troubles we discussed. Unsuccessfully aspiring to become a multiple personality, my patient had not quite completed the split. Instead, as she put it, "Part of me is always watching over my shoulder and ridiculing everything I do. It's Her. She seduces you into being spontaneous and vulnerable, then she smashes you for being weak. Be careful, or she'll kill both of us."

I heard a lot about Her but we did not meet face to face until Cathy and I had spent many hours together and were both deeply engrossed in her account of a particularly frightening violent childhood sexual violation. The molester had tied her up, and told her that she was so sexy no man could resist having her. Emotionally moved by what she had been through, unwittingly and uncharacteristically, I let the hour run over by five minutes. When she realized what had happened, it was Cathy who said, "Our time is up." She hid her upset by teasingly telling me, "See, I even seduced you into giving me extra attention."

When we met for our next therapy session, she was both terrified with what had happened, and furious at me for allowing it. First, in fear, she accused herself of being such a sexy seductress that she got every therapist so turned on that, to feed his perverted fantasies, she had to sacrifice getting the help she sought.

Then she screamed at me in a voice I had not heard before. Alternately, it was aggressively assaulting and mocking disdainful. "You fucked up!" she yelled. "You're the one who's supposed to take care of the time, not me." Then, more coldly deliberate: "I can't believe you're such a baby. Just another sex-starved therapist exploiting patients to feed your fantasies. After I left last time, you probably jerked off thinking about that other asshole tying me up. I hope you heard enough of my problems so you could come."

My attempts to reflect her feelings and interpret her imaginings only seemed to make matters worse. None of my therapeutic interventions slowed her down enough to explore what was terrifying her. At last in desperation I put aside my therapist's role and simply told her about how last session I had felt so touched by the terrible time she'd has a kid, and by her willingness to trust me with her anguish, that I had lost sight of the time.

The tearfulness in my voice was evident. Unexpectedly Cathy responded by lunging toward my throat with bared teeth. Before reaching me, she stopped short, turning her threatened assault on herself by ferociously biting her own arm.

I spoke to her softly but firmly, assuring her that I would always protect her from hurting me. I went on to point out that attending to the time was my job, not hers, and that I would take responsibility for solving whatever problem I was having in doing that. It was only then that she calmed down, and the emotional connection between us that we could usually count on having was restored.

Not sufficiently prepared for an assault by Her, for a moment, I experienced in a small way what it must have been like when, as a trusting child, Cathy had offered herself up, expecting acceptance. Her disdainful dismissal of all I intended, followed by her aborted physical attack, shattered my sense of who I was. In the time it took me to recover, I tasted the terror on which she had been forced to feed.

After that exchange, there was much for us to work out, including other times when we'd both be scared, and again find our relationship at risk. But that time of terror we had gotten through without hurting one another provided a soothing memory to which we could always reassuringly return.

From time to time, we all experience terror in the absence of actual threat. This interaction with Cathy encouraged me to keep in mind that no matter how irrational we may know any particular fear to be, we need to treat our fearful feelings with respect. We may wake in the night in a cold sweat, terrified that we are about to die. Even though we understand that the danger we dread exists only in our imagination, facing the fear may allow us to ask someone we love to hold and comfort us until the terror passes.

Otherwise, like the Grandmother in O'Connor's Gothic tale of terror, by denying the subjective dread from which there is no place to hide, we may increase our risks in other objectively dangerous situations. Or like Cathy, we may live a divided life in which the parts of ourselves we seek to silence come screaming out of the shadows unexpectedly and needlessly endanger both other people and ourselves.

# 7

# Horror and Terror Intertwine to Turn Us Inside Out

The warning list of the seven deadly sins and the moral injunctions of the Ten Commandmants were not formulated for a few bad people. These standards of safety and avoidance of harm were established for everyone.

There are times in each of our lives when we are tempted to commit abominably evil acts. Aspiring to be angels, we may yearn for cosmic experiences to elevate our existence to an ideal of oneness with Universal Love. But in our search for sanctity, the more we ignore the animals we are, the more likely it is that the fearful beast will be released.

During the first few years of my career, I worked in correctional institutions. In each reformatory, prison, and building for the criminally insane, I met some sweet, helpful inmates who seemed too consummately good and obviously innocent to belong behind bars. In every case, it turned out that these seemingly angelic misfits among the clearly criminal apes had either killed someone close to them or had murdered a number of innocent bystanders on a day when the beast within broke loose. In newspaper accounts of their crimes, these one-time kin-killers and the mass-murders of strangers were usually described as "the typical boy next door who was always so kind and polite that it was impossible to imagine he would ever intentionally hurt anyone."

My encounters with these inmates remind me of my meetings with blissed-out gurus and disciples of the spiritual sixties who were so high on meditation, chanting, or some other drug of choice that they believed themselves, everyone else, and the world at large to be perfect just as it was. Unfortunately, their compassion was so impersonal that although they loved everyone and everything in the abstract, their attention was too attached to the ultimate high to be free for concrete personal contact. Often they ignored the suffering of others less fortunate, disparaged their unhappiness as unwarranted, and did not even take decent care of their own children.

I sensed similarities between these two disparate sets of men—the inmates and the gurus. They seemed too good to be true. Their idealized attitudes allowed them to ignore both the horror within themselves and the terrifying threats that await us all in a world that, though not necessarily cruel, need not be nice.

Poe's American Gothic House of Usher horrifies us into unwitting recognition of abhorrent aspects of our seemingly acceptable selves. O'Connor's southern Gothic Misfit terrifies us by arranging an unexpected meeting with appalling events in our otherwise ordinary lives. But there are experiences that fuse our fearful fascination with both horror and terror, that show us what is unacceptable within us and how close to the edge we totter.

Insisting on our innocence, we all build our brightly shining towers on foundations of unlit grottos of guilt. Afraid to find out what we all already know, at times we try to pretend that we are as good and pure as we have been taught we are supposed to be.

When we attempt to keep our pour baser instincts buried in the darkness and silence beneath our conscious awareness, we risk being threatened by the terror that what should be dead will not stay dead. None of us is fully safe from the horror that we could revert to type and respond to the call of the blood. Often the most dangerous people among us are those who are so scared that they cannot admit to themselves that sometimes they could kill.

Oddly enough, not facing our fears may be our most dangerous option. I remember becoming uncomfortably aware of that paradox when my oldest son was still an infant. He wakened late one night and cried out for the third or fourth time. I was sleepy and irritated, but still could not allow myself to accept that I felt mad enough to murder him. Frightened of the fury within me, I was trying very hard to be an ideal parent. This required me to imagine that I was too good a father to become enraged at my own innocent baby.

I was upset that he was not soothed by my soft words. Suddenly I saw that he was terrified. To my horror, I became aware that without consciously intending to, I had handled him roughly.

I realized that I had denied my irritation about his repeated interruption of my sleep over the prior two weeks and now was reacting to that denial. All at once I imagined myself picking my baby up by the heels, swinging him around in the air, and bashing out his brains against the bedroom wall. As I let myself live with that awful image of how murderous I could feel toward my own kid, unexpectedly I felt my body relax. The *worth of imagining that worst possible scenario* was immediately apparent when my son responded immediately to my gentler handling, accepted his bottle, and was soon peacefully asleep.

At that time I was in the army. The following morning, while having coffee with other members of the psychiatric department staff at the base hospital, I told them uneasily of the previous night's eerie interplay between myself and my son.

Several of my military colleagues were also young fathers. A couple of them responded with embarrassment and relief when they confessed equally awful impulses toward their own kids. Only one reacted by self-righteous expression of disgust: "I just don't know how any decent father could want to hurt his own child!" After that exchange, his kid was the only one whose well-being worried me.

As a parent, my worst fear was that I might abuse my own children as my mother had abused me. Swearing to myself that I would never be like her, I had ended up seeing myself simply as the innocent victim of her unwarranted cruelty without acknowledging how frustrating it can sometimes be to take care of kids.

Paradoxically, in trying so hard *not* to be like her, I had risked inadvertently acting out all that I had tried so hard to avoid. It was not until I let go of my idealized self-image and faced my worst fears that I became a better parent more of the time.

If we are to learn how we may best face our fears as grown-ups, we must first understand how we encountered our earliest experiences of alarm as infants. Two other incidents come to mind in the raising of my first child. The first occurred when he was a toddler experiencing fear of the dark. This separation anxiety that threatens eternal abandonment is the emerging developmental prototype of later adult feelings of *horror*.

Understanding my son's reluctance to go to sleep as his fear of separation from access to the security of my protection and aware of my own fears at his age, I comfortably accomodated his needs for reassurance. There were the usual repeated requests for countless drinks of water. We established a ritual of bedtime tales and lullabies told and sung in the same order every night, as well as a preset placement of a company of familiar stuffed animals.

These dependable transitional rites worked well at first. Later on, my son's projected fantasies made him afraid of the child-eating monsters that appeared under his bed whenever I turned out the lights. This apprehension of annihilation that threatens to emerge from the child's unknown outside world is the early developmental prototype of an eventual adult *terror* that I know too well in myself.

Nightlights and earlier rituals proved ineffective to dispel my son's fear of specters lurking in the shadows. I made him a toy sword, taught him how to use it to fend off phantoms, and laid it beside his pillow each night. We were both relieved when his newfound power to defend himself allowed him to fall asleep more easily. Each morning he awoke with delightful breakfast tales of monsters slain the previous night.

Eventually the monsters came no more. Soon my son was old enough to venture about boldly and to begin climbing trees. Well aware of my own irrational fear of heights and unwilling to burden my son with the same fear, I stood close enough to catch him if he fell, kept my apprehensions to myself, and openly shared his delight in mastering the limitations of gravity.

When we take care of helplessly vulnerable children, our own hidden horror and terror resonates in response to theirs. No matter how awful it may seem to some of us, we must learn to accept that we are at least as much apes, as we are angels. Otherwise, like the other murderers I've met, we leave unattended the baser instincts that we are afraid to acknowledge. Without warning, they may sneak up behind us.

Relatively few of us actually end up murdering other people. We may, however, carelessly mistreat them because we deny our fears and idealize our images of who we are in ways that limit our empathy and compassion for those we care about. Enraptured by our interest in more important matters of the spirit, some of us may put off meeting our children's needs for personal attention. When we do, we not only risk becoming spiritually inadequate angels; worse yet, we don't even offer the natural parenting of biologically healthy apes.

We waste too much time immersed in anxiety about whether we are good or bad. We might be better off expending our energy on simply taking care of all that needs doing. A tale is told of a young Buddhist monk who worried a lot. While walking through the forest to return to his monastery he came upon an old Zen master. Delighted to have found an audience for his obsessions, he tried to strike up a conversation with this seemingly carefree older man.

The young monk talked a great deal, mostly about himself. The old man listened and smiled, but did not seem to have much to say. In the midst of his monologue, the young man declared, "I became a monk to attain spiritual enlightenment. For a long while I was afraid I would never attain a saintly attitude, but my years of spiritual sacrifice have paid off and now I have become quite humble."

"How about you?" he asked the old man, "Are you humble?"

After a few moments of quiet concentration, the master replied, "I don't really know. I've never thought much about it."

Three

# Courage and Caring

# 8

# Proceed with Caution, or Just Get on with It?

Our fears need not dominate our lives. If something frightening beckons, we can choose to accept the invitation or to decline. Each of us has to take responsibility for deciding when to risk and when to run. The situation itself often indicates the safest and sanest ways of dealing with that particular danger.

We don't have to avoid adventure altogether and miss out on much of the fun that freedom allows. By considering all of our options for coping with fright, we expand the possibilities for living courageously in an unsafe world. Although we sometimes must make choices in situations where outcomes are uncertain, it's not always necessary to choose blindly between reckless abandon and cautious construction. We might best begin by establishing some guidelines for when it's better to take bold action and when cautious inaction offers an advantage.

When faced with a fearful decision, most of us are likely to procrastinate. While we wait to decide what to do next, our anxiety builds. To relieve the mounting tension, we feel tempted to ignore warnings of impending harm and take the plunge. Some of us are tempted to retreat and run. Quickly, we remember how often reckless risk results in disaster. Once more, we decide to remain undecided.

Reading horror stories is one thing; facing life's horrors is another. We find the thrill of fiction in our uncertainty about the story's outcome, just as in life, when we are willing to forego certainty in favor of the enjoyment of surprises, the suspense may make life more exciting. Although the frightening incidents of everyday life are usually more ordinary than in horror fiction, uncertainty about their outcome can make us just as uncomfortable.

Too much tension, however, can transform the pleasure of vibrant expectation into the stress of deadly apprehension. When we are sitting around a campfire awaiting the delayed denouement of a ghost story, we may feel delight. But in our daily lives, when we drag our feet indecisively as a way of putting off the outcome of an intended action, we end up feeling depressed.

By way of example, I offer an unnecessarily long experience of alarm I suffered when I was about ten years old. The city had opened a public swimming pool near enough to my home for me to reach by bus on my own. It was wonderful—overcrowded and excessively chlorinated—but wonderful. During that summer, whenever I could, I spent the entire day at the pool. Gradually overcoming my fears, I tried swimming in deeper and deeper water, and jumping off higher and higher diving boards. The only challenge I felt too frightened to take on was the seemingly sky-high slide into the pool.

It took most of that summer for me to line up behind the other kids who climbed the long metal ladder. It led to an elevated platform from which they launched their whirlwind slide into the water below. Late in August, I finally got as far as the platform, but I could not bring myself to attempt the terrifying descent.

74

Almost immediately after I reached the platform, I realized there was no safe way down. The ladder steps were blocked by a line of kids one behind the other from the platform to the ground.

I felt absolutely paralyzed. Despite the cruel jeering of the other children. I sat sniveling in a corner of the platform. After almost two hours of clinging to the rail, and shivering from outer chill and inner cowardice, my shame finally outweighed my fear. I said a prayer, took a deep breath, and suicided down the slide.

The daring adventure was both easier and more exciting than I could have imagined. I spent the rest of the day climbing up the steps and sliding down into the pool.

When I finally got home, I told my father about all I had been through. It reminded him of an awful experience of his own when he was my age. Although it still made him uncomfortable, he told me all about it.

He had grown up as one of many children of an immigrant family who lived in poverty in the New York City slum known as Hell's Kitchen. Until they grew too tall to fit, the kids slept crosswise, six to a bed. My father was full grown and on his own before he had any clothes bought just for him. Before that, for his birthday, he was given a haircut at the barbershop.

Before he was old enough to get a regular job, he fulfilled his financial responsibilities to the family by going down to the docks to throw stones at the men who worked on the passing coal barges. In retaliation, they threw lumps of coal at him. He then gathered up the pieces in a burlap sack and brought them home to heat the family's tenement apartment coal stove. When he finished sixth grade, he had to quit school to take a paid job hauling garbage.

The story he told me was of a winter afternoon when he was still in school. He had been given a nickel and told to take a long detour on his way home to go to a bakery that sold day-old bread for two cents. By the time he got back to the house, he was very cold. There were no overcoats in the family. Instead he was wearing a hand-me-down, six-pocketed, homemade sweater.

Once back on his own block, my father was suddenly scared that he might have lost the three cents change. His father was certain to beat him. Even if the loss went undetected, there was so little money to feed the family that he would have felt guilty about going unpunished.

He began looking through his six sweater pockets. As he discovered that one after another was empty, his panic grew. By the time he reached the house, there was only one pocket left unexplored. He was so scared that it too would turn out to be empty that he could not bring himself to test out this last desperate hope. Instead he sat out on the stoop for hours.

The day grew colder and so did my father, but he was just too frightened to look and see whether or not the change was in that last pocket. Because he could not face finding out that he might have lost those three pennies, he could not allow himself to learn if he had not. I no longer remember how the story turned out, but I have never forgotten the image of him shivering in the cold because he was unable to face his fear, nor will I ever forget my father's generosity in telling me his story.

As we hesitate at the threshold of a frightening dilemma, *the best touchstone for taking action is whether or not our delaying further will make the situation any safer*. As an example, consider a time when at last you received a long awaited letter of reply to an application for a desperately needed job. Delaying its opening out of fear of rejection is a waste of time, an extension of needless anxiety, and an exercise in futility.

There is no use kidding ourselves that waiting a while will make us any more ready later than we feel right now. It is already time to take the plunge of opening the envelope. None of us will ever feel fully prepared to face the unknown. Often, when we decide not to decide, waiting only makes us more anxious. We might as well set aside our excuses as soon as we can, take a deep breath, and get on with our lives.

There are other scary situations in which *delay allows us to rethink the parameters of the dangers we face*, for example when we make decisions about undergoing surgery or undertaking major career changes. Cautious consideration works better than impulsive action.

When we delay deciding on a course of action in that sort of uncertain situation, our hesitation may allow us to imagine more sensible alternatives. Having taken time to figure out what is likely to work best, we can act boldly.

If instead, we rush into such situations, ignoring warnings of clear and imminent danger, we usually do so out of willful insistence on getting our own way. Demonically driven, we may unintentionally increase the likelihood of the jeopardy we fear. *It is foolish to rush recklessly ahead simply because we insist (incorrectly) that we just can't stand feeling so nervous.*

Adolescence is a time of this sort of reckless impulsiveness. During my teenage years, I often acted incautiously out of impatience. I couldn't wait long enough to figure out how best to get what I wanted, or to consider any dangerous consequences. However, my motive was less likely to be the pursuit of passion with which I felt possessed, than the avoidance of whatever anxiety I experienced as unbearable.

As a boy growing into manhood in the forties, I was attempting to establish a pre-feminist macho image that would only later have its self-consciousness raised. During the summer of my sixteenth year, boys in the Bronx still believed that a girl either *did*, or she *didn't*. A girl-who-did would be willing to get laid by any boy bold enough to approach her, while a girl-who-didn't would

77

allow only one boy to make love to her, but not until after they were married.

Boys were different. At that age, no matter how often we jerked off, our penises were perpetually erect, and we were ever on the lookout for places to put them. We talked a lot about getting laid. Mostly we lied about it. Even if we were with a girl who everyone knew did not go all the way, our fear of being summarily dismissed in the hallway outside her apartment door was mainly of our embarrassment about what to tell the guys back on the corner.

That summer I was the next to the last one in my crowd who was still a virgin. My determination to change all that as soon as possible was not as much a sexual issue as it was anxiety about my inferior social status. I insisted that before my next birthday, I would find a girl with whom I could have my way, or I would die trying.

Summers offered an opportunity to escape from my parents' intrusive restrictions on my freedom. The previous year, when they decided to stay at home in the city, I made sure to get a job in the country. The following summer, my parents planned to vacation in a rented cottage in the Catskill Mountains. Knowing that their cottage was near the resort hotel at which I had worked the summer before, I turned down my option to return to my old job. Instead I went to an urban employment agency and got placed as a counter-busboy at the Waldorf-Astoria Hotel in midtown New York City.

A counter-busboy brings food from the hotel kitchen to the upper echelon staff dining room, and later returns the dirty dishes to the clean-up area. At the time, the Waldorf had a selectively stratified ethnic distribution of employees. The administrative staff members were all American-born WASPs, the chefs were all French, and the bakers were German, while the dishwashing and janitorial employees were all Puerto Rican immigrants. We counter-busboys were a cosmopolitan assortment of young second- and third-generation Irish, Italian, and Jewish Americans.

The Puerto Ricans kept mostly to themselves, intimately speaking Spanish, colorfully gesticulating, laughing and horsing around a lot. Through my sixteen-year-old Jewish eyes, they looked freer and happier than I had ever been. All the swarthy young men appeared strong, suave, and at ease with their wild, wild women.

No wonder that they were so free of apparent anxiety. It was unmistakably clear to me that every exotically attractive *señorita* was definitely a girl-who-did. For the first time, I was everlastingly grateful to Mr. Rosenberg, the junior high school teacher who had worked so hard to teach me to speak Spanish.

I tried out my limited foreign language skills on a seductive older woman, a Puerto Rican dishwasher named Maria who must have been at least twenty. She had a tough, impressively muscular younger brother named Manuel. I had once heard him warn off another counter-busboy he had spotted flirting with Maria. Manuel was convincingly threatening about killing the boy if he did not stay away from his sister.

With my pride set on getting laid, I ignored the danger implied in his warnings. Fortunately, when I first flirted with Maria, Manuel seemed not to notice me. After our first contact, she saw to it that we had time alone in the hotel alcoves, hallways, and cleaning supply closets. We hugged and kissed, and fooled around. I had too little Spanish, and she too little English, for either of us to say much more than that we loved each other. Except by touch, we never got to know one another.

By the summer's end, Maria had given me her address, and set a time for me to visit when none of her many relatives would be at home. At the appointed hour, without worrying about entering the neighborhood, I went to her tenement apartment in Spanish Harlem. I discounted the menacing stares of the unemployed young men who hung around rightfully resenting any unwanted strangers who invaded their territory.

After this first tryst with Maria, I hurried home to my own Bronx neighborhood to announce to the guys on the corner the triumph of finally having gotten laid. When I got to work at the Waldorf on the following day I was exhilarated enough to foolishly throw caution to the winds.

Although I saw that Manuel was watching us, I flirted openly with Maria. He cornered me against the kitchen wall. Held in the terrible grip of his powerful fist, I found my foreign language comprehension even more limited than usual. Combined with his fury, my fright made Manuel's rapid-fire Spanish almost unintelligible. When he did not actually hurt me, I understood that he had not yet heard that I had been in his home having sex with his sister. Pulling out a switchblade knife, he began speaking more slowly and clearly. He warned me that if I ever bothered his sister again, he was going to cut off my cock and stuff it in my mouth.

Evidently, he never did find out what had gone on between Maria and me. I never spoke to her again, nor she to me. I felt hurt that she could give me up so easily, but mostly I felt relieved that her brother had not carried out his frightening threat. In a willfully reckless way, I had impatiently insisted on ignoring warnings of danger. By acting impulsively to announce the attainment of my manhood, I had risked losing it forever.

Instead of taking the time to think carefully about my choices and their consequences, I acted impulsively. If I had taken the time to consider my safety, I could have met Maria on less dangerous turf, hidden our relationship from her menacingly protective brother, and still gotten laid.

Uncertainty can make all of us anxious from time to time. When we sort out our apprehensions, some seem irrational while others indicate actual danger. Facing our fears lets us tell the difference between those times when delaying our decision to act improves our chances of emerging unharmed and those times when procrastinating simply prolongs our anxiety.

It is not a matter of moderation. The only issue we need consider is which way of biting the bullet will work best in a particular situation. *It takes one kind of courage to wait patiently, and another to get on with it.*

# When We're Scared, Sometimes We Hold on Too Tight

Early psychological theorists studied animal behavior and summarily settled the issue of how human beings cope with fear by assigning it the simplistic formula: fight or flight. When we are stuck between danger on the one side and safety on the other, this works as an easy and accurate description of our personal alternatives to just staying scared. We can either attack in an effort to destroy or drive off the danger, or attempt to escape to some safer place or protective person.

But in some situations, the threat of danger and the promise of safety come from the same source. Children who suffer poor parenting are afraid of the only people to whom they can turn for protection. Emotionally unprepared for a forced choice between dominating or departing, the helplessly dependent child is unlikely to survive the outcome of either alternative.

Grown-ups sometimes face the adult equivalent of these childhood dilemmas. Although such encounters may not seem as powerful as the struggles between parent and child, our conflicts are similarly difficult to resolve. When scared, we often seek the support and protection of our spouses, our closest friends, or our bosses.

We have all known times when the people we counted on most for comfort also posed the greatest threat to our well-being. When we are threatened by people we depend on, if we fight back, we risk being abandoned, rejected, or fired. If instead of fighting, we choose to flee, we risk finding ourselves alone, friendless, or out of work.

Faced with dangerous dilemmas as complex as these, we discover that they do not readily yield to simple solutions. Among the strategies some of us use to extricate ourselves from these intricate anxieties are *Attachment*, *Isolation*, and *Merger*, which can be formulated as slogans:

> *Attachment*: "If you can't win, learn to love losing."
> *Isolation*: "If you can't run away, withdraw into fantasy."
> *Merger*: "If living your own life is too scary, lose yourself in the crowd."

All three adaptations appear in sequence during ordinary early childhood development. *Attachment* is expressed in a child's learning to adapt to mother's mishandling as if it were an acceptable expression of attention.[1] *Isolation* requires that the child hide its own needs in exchange for the security afforded by satisfying the mother's wishes. *Merger* involves emotional accommodation to whatever is expected, as if the child has no separate self of its own. In most children, each strategy emerges as part of a phase that eventually passes.

Under extreme stress, any of these otherwise phase-appropriate adaptations can become a desperate defense. The child experiences one or more of these tactics as necessary for emotional survival in a frightening family situation that cannot otherwise be escaped. In this chapter, we explore the strategy of Attachment.

Rather than risk separation, a child must sometimes

settle for a less than satisfactory response from its mother. But if criticism is the only kind of attention a child can expect, it may learn to always settle for negative attention, and even begin to invite scolding by purposely behaving in ways that annoy the critical parents.

At its best, the child's attachment to the mother later serves as a basis for feeling a safe bond of affection in adult love relationships. But some children have had to attach emotionally to a mother who is otherwise uninterested. If this remains their way of coping with their fear of deprivation, they grow into adults who will avoid doing things on their own, preferring instead to cling to others in a helplessly dependent way. Although these children originally establish this attachment with their mothers to avoid abandonment, as passively attached adults, they are likely to pair with partners who abuse the power that dependent people give them. Ironically, the threat of separation that the dependent person fears and had hoped to banish remains in the picture.

Imagine how frightening it must be for an infant who finds that the parent on whom it counts for protection is also the danger against which defense is needed. The infant must *either accept whatever is offered or learn to do without anything at all*.

By the time they become toddlers, infants take on as their own any response repeatedly offered as comfort during their early mothering. For example, in an attempt to ease an infant's agitation, some mothers bounce their crying babies. Consequently as its own way of reacting to fear faced alone, the excessively bounced baby becomes an overly active child.

What was once the mother's inappropriate attempt to pacify then becomes the child's own preferred choice of self-comforting behavior. These children are unable to take good care of themselves, and their chronic agitation invites retaliatory reactions from other children.

After a while, it seems that everyone has joined forces to push them around.

Later in life, they persist in their unfortunate attachment to abuse and selectively increase the probability of picking a partner who will mistreat them. These martyred adults sometimes sound strangely soothed when they complain about how badly they are treated by the people they love. Often they express satisfaction in their endless accounts of unfair treatment on the job by bosses whose employ they are unlikely to leave. This seemingly masochistic adult behavior is an extension of the panicky attachment they acquired as infants who learned to adapt to otherwise inescapable abuse.

In modern horror fiction, this particular capacity for coping with anxiety is chillingly portrayed in William Faulkner's famous short story, "A Rose for Emily."[2] Characteristically, Faulkner kept violence and the grotesque at the center of his stories, but unlike other southern Gothic authors, the way he portrayed horror was intended to illustrate how much the human spirit is able to endure and still survive.

In this story, Emily's unique style of attachment sustains her in the face of anxiety so overwhelming that it would otherwise have done her in. Her strange solution at first seems alien to anything we ourselves would ever consider, but in reading Faulkner's bizarre tale, we risk realizing how much like Emily we all are.

The narrator begins by telling about the time the whole town turned out to attend Miss Emily's funeral. Some folks showed up as an expression of respect for the reclusive maiden lady, but most came out of curiosity about the decaying house in which she had for so long hidden herself away.

Miss Emily's father had been an authoritarian aristocrat who drove away her suitors with his horsewhip. None of the young men was ever quite good enough for his daughter. For three days after his death, Miss

Emily had insisted that her father was still alive and had refused to allow his body to be buried.

It took Miss Emily another two years before she permitted herself to pick a sweetheart—a northern day laborer her father would have abhorred. The town expected them to marry; instead, one day Miss Emily's fiance suddenly vanished. She withdrew into spinsterish seclusion once again, entombed in the deteriorating house of her dead father till her hair turned iron grey.

Many years earlier, out of respect for Miss Emily's dead father, the mayor had written off the family's unpaid taxes. Several days after the disappearance of her fiance, the town aldermen arrived at the house and attempted to collect these remitted monies. She faced down the aldermen as successfully as she had the town druggist from whom she had purchased poison the previous week. They gave in, and left too intimidated to mention the mysterious smell that permeated the old mansion.

Faulker's story ends as it began, with Miss Emily's death. She died downstairs. Although the townspeople were particularly curious about an upstairs room that none of them had seen for forty years, their sense of decency demanded that they wait until after her burial before forcing the door.

Once inside, they were astonished to discover a bridal bedroom delicately decorated with rose-colored curtains and rose-shaded lights. Carefully arranged on the dressing table lay a man's toilet articles, and on a chair beside the table hung his neatly folded suit. On the bed lay the man himself.

His skull displayed a "fleshless grin." His body, or at least, "what was left of him, rotted beneath what was left of the night-shirt . . . [In a second pillow beside his own was] . . . the indentation of a head . . . [and a single] . . . long strand of iron-grey hair."[3]

\* \* \*

Miss Emily's fear of abandonment was so unbearable that she would not allow her lover to leave. Frightened because he seemed inaccessible to her, she killed him so she could cling to his corpse. Rather than face the horror of living unprotected and alone, she made her own macabre marital bed and slept in it.

Her pattern of coping with fear of abandonment is not entirely unlike that of a woman who came to me for therapy. Although less bizarre than Miss Emily's, Vicky's strategies constituted an equally self-destructive, extended attachment to abusive parenting. She suffered what for her was an incomprehensible, lifelong depression, ameliorated only by increasing addiction to drugs prescribed by a psychiatrist. Underlying this symptomatic complaint was an agonized life-style. From early adolescence on, Vicky had lived with a series of husbands and lovers who had abused her physically and emotionally.

Working with me was not her first experience in psychotherapy, but she presented herself as a pathetically helpless creature who could not possibly know what to do or say unless I instructed her. Hoping to demonstrate that I did not take her seeming helplessness so seriously, I pointed out how she passively directed me to take care of her. In refusing to accept her clinging as the weakness she claimed it expressed, I interpreted her attachment as an aggressive attempt to control her access to me.

In response, Vicky immediately brightened up to compliment me on "the straightforwardness of that perceptive insight." At last she had found a therapist "bright enough to see through my style and not let me get away with that stuff." Seductively, she told me that she found my "abrasiveness" appealing, but warned me that though she wished to be directed, she would not stand for my telling her how to live her life.

Vicky described both her eccentric father and her

hysterical mother as "authoritarian." Mother's martyrdom was a consequence of an "insane submissiveness" to Father's "sane tyranny," so she felt justified in battering Vicky whenever the child behaved in any way that made her anxious.

Father made Vicky spend many hours doing chores after school every day. At the same time, he expected high academic achievement. But it was easier to submit to his exhausting expectations than to meet Mother's insatiable hunger for sympathy for her suffering and the sacrifices she claimed to have made. Compared to Mother's madness, with which the child could not cope, Father's excessive demands for excellence came as a relief.

Neither parent ever seemed satisfied with their daughter's attempts to please them. In response to Vicky's best efforts, her father often expressed his dissatisfaction in the form of ridicule, followed by cold withdrawal. When Mother was displeased, she cried, screamed, and beat Vicky with a leather strap until the child's legs bled. Both parents threatened to banish her from a home in which there was "no place for a girl who didn't care enough to do as she was told."

As a child, the only personal attention Vicky received from either parent was abuse intended to improve her character enough so that she would no longer deserve to be abandoned. As a woman, she repeatedly became involved with men who wanted to improve her. At the outset, she often was intuitively aware of their "ambivalence." They all eventually turned out to be impossible to satisfy. When we discussed her early sensitivity to the threats these men posed, Vicky felt bewildered by how often she had ignored the warnings rather than risk separation.

She always tried to imagine that the abusive men she repeatedly picked as partners were better than she knew them to be. It was hard for her to give up hoping that, if only she could become whatever it was that they wanted her to be, then they would be sufficiently satisfied to treat her well. Occasionally she would meet a "decent" man, and sometimes accept him as a friend, but romantic attachment was reserved for those who treated her badly.

The absence of social amenities in my treatment of Vicky, coupled with my unapologetic observations about her actions and attitudes, sometimes made her feel that I was rude and uncaring. Several times, halfway through a session, Vicky left the office in tears. She always returned determined to "try to do better."

I understood her threatened abandonment of therapy as a warning that if I didn't care enough to do as I was told, there would be no place for me in her life. Because I see stubbornness as strength that has not yet been let loose, my respect for Vicky's obstinate attachment was enough to warrant my sticking with her. It seemed worth risking the danger that someday when she walked out in the middle of one of our meetings, she might decide never to return.

Residual attachment to the unforgiving mother of my own childhood made it easier for me to accept the risk. Before I was old enough to enter kindergarten, I had already been warned that she might have to send me to reform school, and in any case, my incorrigible attitudes would someday put me behind bars.

Instead, somehow I made my way through public school as a very bright but uncontrollable problem child. I muddled through college as well, and on into graduate school, softening my irascible nature by staying high on grass much of the time. Eventually, by becoming a psychological intern in a reformatory for young adult male felons, I fulfilled the family prophecy by ending up in prison.

At the time, I was still attached to imagining that my becoming a professional man would at last please my mother. I had not yet fully realized that she found it impossible ever to feel satisfied. Instead her chronic disappointment was once again evident when she pointed out to me that a Ph.D. was not a *real* doctor.

She went on to complain that she couldn't even show anyone what was in the coffee-table copy of her son's dissertation because the case study texts contained dirty words. In any case, she had been right all along that I would end up in prison. Although it was true that I was there as a staff member, it was also true that I still wasted my time "hanging around with bums and low-lifes."

Like Vicky, I was so afraid of being abandoned as unfit for human company that I went on atoning for unearned guilt over not having cured my mother's depression. For several years longer than was worth my while, I went on serving my time in correctional institutions. By the time Vicky and I met, I had not yet granted myself a full pardon. But unlike Vicky, I had at least gotten a stay of execution, a parole into private practice, and a probationary period in which I was trying to learn to adjust to an easier life.

When Vicky first came to see me, she kept returning home to give her family another chance, although she had already begun to recognize the damage done to her. After all, she argued, these were the only parents she would ever get to have. The idea of simply doing without seemed more than she could bear. Also, at any cost, she wanted to avoid her most awful conscious dread of turning out to be as unfair as her demanding father, or as cruel as her dissatisfied mother. Early in life, she had vowed never to act like either one.

Ironically, the ways in which she attempted to avoid emulating their abusiveness encouraged the aggressiveness that she most feared both from her father and her mother. Often her own interactions with other people ended up as an unwitting parody of the parental attitudes she abhorred.

Vicky worked hard all day as a bright, resourceful, and successful professional journalist. When she got home and was ready to relax, her lover would ask her to type his papers. Again and again, she would comply, passively encouraging him to demand more and more of her.

Eventually, she would martyr herself enough to prove that her lover only wanted to use her without really caring about her needs. Once she had demonstrated what a selfish bastard he was, she could ridicule him openly and withdraw after cruelly shredding his papers to ribbons. At that point, she could say no, leave him, and begin the cycle again with some other "sadistic male chauvinist."

She did not feel justified in striking back until after she had suffered enough martyrdom to merit concern for her own needs. When her private vindictiveness could no longer be contained, in an ugly amalgam of Father's mockery and Mother's rage, Vicky put forth a tirade aimed at publicly humiliating any abusive partner who had "taken advantage" of her good nature.

In the course of therapy, she became aware of how she unwittingly set herself up for unnecessary abuse. As she learned to heed previously ignored signs of danger, she was more often able to avoid becoming attached to men who were likely to hurt her.

Previously, if a man stood her up or came very late to their first date, she always gave him another chance. Now she began to take early signs of neglect as clear indicators of later unhappiness. When a man was inconsiderate, or unfairly demanding, she learned to confront him immediately. If he was not conciliatory, she could more quickly terminate the relationship without having to go through the suffering to which her previous attachments had subjected her.

Whenever she could overcome her fear that operating out of self-interest meant that she was as cruelly selfish as her parents, Vicky found that she could stand her ground. Each self-affirming assertion made the next one easier. As a result, her depression began to lift without dependence on drugs. Gradually, her attachment to abusive men became less frequent, did not last as long, and was no longer the center of what was once an unhappy life.

But Vicky was still unable to escape the panicky feeling that someday she would end up unwanted and alone. This frightening fantasy involved an image of herself as a homeless bag lady, wandering the streets of Washington, garnering scraps from garbage cans, and getting mugged and raped by bands of marauding men.

Recognizing that her fear of vulnerable vagrancy was "unreal," she insisted that if only she knew how she would do anything to rid herself of this irrational dread. I suggested that this dreadful fantasy served as a defense to mask some horror even more awful than her obsession with abandonment. She reacted by telling me she no longer felt that she could count on me to understand her and to be on her side. Instead, she angrily accused me of badgering her unfairly.

When I went on to suggest that she was once again experiencing in me those awful aspects of her parents that she could not bear to recognize in herself, Vicky was outraged. But for the first time, she did not collapse into tears and leave because I had hurt her. No matter how angry at me she had become, she felt strong and independent enough to stay. I told her that what she secretly feared most was true: she *had* acquired those aspects of her parents that she hated most. It was then that Vicky's rage really exploded in an unchecked verbal assault.

I was silent for what seemed a long while. After a time, I acknowledge that for a few moments, my reaction had been to experience the frightening old feeling that my mother was right after all about me: I was unfit for human company. I told her how often my mother had explained her constant criticism as an effort to improve me enough for other people to be able to bear being around me.

During those moments of seemingly unspeakable emotion, I admitted I had hated Vicky enough to want to strangle her. I had even imagined for a moment that my murdering her would be for her own good. Vicky was relieved to learn that now I seldom suffer either that horror or my murderous rage.

I cried a little. Vicky cried a lot. Working through her horror took many more sessions. Neither of us ever forgot the time when we realized that although our worst fears about ourselves were true, together we could face them. Our horror of being abandoned no longer required us to take abuse we did not deserve. The parts of ourselves we had imagined to be so awful that their exposure would make anyone else want to leave us to die—unprotected and alone—no longer had to be hidden.

We can all come to realize that although our worst horrors about ourselves are in some sense true, other people in our adult lives need not find them as awful as our parents once did. Even if some people cannot stand something about us that is truly awful, there are others we can turn to. In any case, whatever some people may disapprove of, is not all there is to us.

Exposing an inner dimension we have hidden away for a lifetime doesn't have to be the end of the world. If we want to face our fear of destroying the people we depend on, we may have to reveal how murderous we sometimes feel. But we can do this without actually killing the ones we love, and even without hurting their feelings.

It is one thing to attack someone physically, or even

to threaten to do so. It is a very different experience for both people when we bracket our awful feelings within the caring that continues. Even after a really awful argument, it's possible to say softly, "I hate how much I hate you at times like these. Because you mean so much to me, I get frightened when I'm tempted to destroy you. I'm still scared that now that you know this about me, you won't ever want to have anything more to do with me."

When we face the fear we have coped with so long by avoidant attachment, as adults we are once again able to surrender willingly to our deepest feelings. Instead of one of us having to lose and learning to love it, amazingly enough, we both can win. I am still astonished every time someone I love can hear the caring intended in my awful confessions.

# Sometimes We Get So Scared, We Have to Hide Who We Are

When we were small children just learning to cope with fear, we first had to make sure we would be safe enough to survive. *Attachment* to our parents protected us from harm. If they were emotionally reliable, then we learned to be hopeful about later love relationships. But if our earliest experiences of protection also subjected us to the danger of separation, then we grew up afraid that the adult partners we picked would also threaten to leave us.

Our longing for a secure personal sense of self came second only to our need to feel safe enough to survive. We needed selves of our own about which we could feel good. If our parents treated us as worthy of respect in our own right, then by the time we grew up, we felt at ease in revealing ourselves and expected that some people would be pleased to know who we were.

But if we had parents who were unaccepting of our independent identities, we learned to hide who we really were for fear that we were not allowed to be ourselves. We created the illusion that all we wanted was to fulfill our parents' needs. In the safety of *Isolation* from parental intrusions, we sustained a secret self.

We coped with childhood fears by hiding what we really felt, and grew up afraid that unless we met other people's expectations, they would reject us.

If our isolation endures into our adult years, no matter how anxious to please we may seem on the surface, we remain secretly disdainful and aloof. Although we often show off as if we feel that we are something special, inside we feel unworthy of the attention we invite. We are easily offended because, beneath our display of arrogance, we feel like frauds.

Those of us who get caught up in negative attachments are held hostage by our horror that if we expose some awful aspect of ourselves, others may abandon us. Those of us who cope with fear by isolating who we are live in terror that if other people knew we had selves of our own, they would destroy us for daring to exist independent of them. We seek security by trying to impress other people so that they will let us live. We don't really care about what anyone else experiences, but their confirmation serves to ward off our fear of annihilation.

Nowhere in modern tales of terror is isolation portrayed more touchingly than in Eudora Welty's "Clytie." This short story exposes the illusions within which we sometimes obscure our identities, and intensifies our anxiety about the exorbitant price we pay for hiding out. This is not just a matter of imagination, she insists, "life is strange, stories hardly make it more so, they [only] make it more believably, more inevitably so." [2]

Originally, Welty found her creative imagination a safe haven from a life too terrifying to meet head-on. Eventually she found the courage to reengage the outside world. She describes herself as "a writer who came of a sheltered life [but] a sheltered life can be a daring life as well. For all serious daring starts from within." [3]

Although anti-heroine Clytie Farr hides herself from

the intrusions of her aggressively overbearing family, unlike Ms. Welty, she is not able to break through to the world of other people. In the end, the secret self sustained by Clytie's isolation is a sad and empty fantasy.

Remnants of a once-prominent small town southern family, the Farrs live in an almost unfurnished mansion and try to project an image of themselves as "too good to associate with other people." The dark and barren interior of the house has long remained closed to the "common" people who consider the Farrs' patrician attitudes peculiar and absurd. Like its owners, the decaying house has "everything locked up absolutely tight." With every shade pulled down, and every window closed and locked, they maintain the illusion that everything is safe.

Within the seeming security of this aristocratic asylum, Clytie takes care of all the others. A half-crazed older sister tyrannically screams down orders from her seclusion on the second floor. A demanding depressed younger brother is too alcoholically exhausted to take care of himself. Clytie's endless responsibilities also include seeing to an eccentric father whose innate irritability has been exaggerated by a paralyzing stroke. She is spared having to tend to an older brother who committed suicide by shooting himself in the head. Surrendered to a life of family service, she has given up everything except her secret fantasies about who she will someday become.

The story opens with Clytie's daily afternoon escape from isolation, going to town. She no longer pretends to be on an urgent errand and no one bothers to speak to her. The townspeople hide their smirks while whispering to each other about this gawky frump of a spinster. They do not know that Clytie sees herself as someone special who awaits the smile that will assure her of her worth.

She is a Cinderella whose prince never comes. But as each day passes and she grows increasingly frightened and alienated, she still stubbornly insists that everything is "nice." Clytie continues to search for the face of her dreams—a half-remembered, happy face with "an open, serene, trusting expression." Any open display of her own outrage and unhappiness Clytie keeps to herself, cursing and crying only when she is alone. Left speechless in her isolation, she never says aloud to other family members that she really feels: "If you do that again, I'll have to kill you!"

The story ends when the older sister once again berates Clytie for doing something on her own and their brother complains about the noise she is making. Instead of fetching rain-water for Papa's shave, Clytie has run to the rain barrel seeking something for herself. As if grateful for an opportunity to embrace an old friend, she wraps her arms around the barrel.

Looking into the wavering rainwater, Clytie thinks she sees the face she has been looking for so long. Terrified by its unexpected ugliness and signs of suffering, she recoils in shock:

The brows were drawn together as if in pain, the eyes intent, almost avid, the nose discolored as if from weeping, the mouth old and closed from any speech.[4]

Too late to save her life, Clytie recognizes the face in the barrel as her own. In the isolation of her imagination, she is still the loving, laughing person she once was, but in the reflected image of the rainwater, she sees the old, ugly, unhappy creature she has become.

It is more dreadful than Clytie can bear. And so she did the only thing she could think of to do. As if impatiently grateful for an opportunity to embrace an old friend, she bent her angular body further, and thrust her head into the barrel, under the water and held it there. When [they] found her, she had fallen forward into the barrel, with her poor ladylike black-stockinged legs up-ended and hung apart like a pair of tongs.[5]

Doomed to live in a house filled with hatred, Clytie could not discover her identity. The sudden shattering of this pathetic victim's idealized illusion about who she was left her with no escape except suicide. Neither the mythological Narcissus nor Clytie died for having fallen in love with themselves. In desperation, each was destined to the doomed pursuit of an unattainably idealized phantom lover.

To escape the dangerous personal intrusions of a family that did not want to know who she was, Clytie created an unreal inner world in which she had a wonderful secret self who would someday be saved. But following a fantasy figure only isolated her further from whatever else she might have gotten out of the life on the edge of which she almost lived.

One of the most isolated people I ever met was a patient of mine I will call Isaac. Although he explained his seeking psychotherapy as an attempt to resolve his indecision about entering graduate school, early on, he said of himself: "I don't identify with my life."

His lack of a clearly defined sense of who he was made every decision a dilemma. He had taken aptitude examinations for graduate school because that was what he was supposed to do when he neared completing college. But when he scored so high that the preferred schools offered him early admission as well as large scholarship grants, he refused to enter because he did not know if that was where he belonged.

During our first session, Isaac began by challenging

the pressure he expected I would put on him to go to graduate school. For the first five minutes he delivered a stubbornly opinionated and searing critique of his career choice and how it would corrupt his ideals. For the next five minutes, he discredited this strong stand and obsequiously apologized for imagining that he knew what was best for him.

From there on, Isaac trailed off into a discussion of the impossibility of establishing any personal meaning in a world that "undoes individuality." In the safety and isolation of his highly idiosyncratic imaginings, he had developed a hard-to-follow, elaborate "religio-aesthetic" theory of the purity of higher mathematics. At times it allowed him some relief from his terror of intimacy with other people by proving that meaningful personal interaction was an absolute impossibility.

During these nihilistically reassuring moments. Isaac felt certain there could be no contact with other people. But it did not take him long to destroy this defense by apologetically dismissing his own ideas. Insisting that he was an unrealistic fool who knew nothing, he disavowed his idiosyncratic, abstract mathematical model for life, and in its place put his parents' practical politics of dollars-and-sense economics. Unable to decide whose ideas he would follow, he was incapable of choosing a career.

He agonized over the act of entering therapy, first by demonstrating that he had a mind of his own, and then by making it clear that if he needed my help in deciding how he should live, his mind must have "turned to mush." This contradiction confused him even more when his attention shifted back to his wealthy family's intrusive expectations.

"I know I should be grateful to them for paying for my therapy," he began. But after tasting that emotion for a moment, Isaac spit it out in disgust, saying, "My parents have often indulged me, but there are always strings attached that strangle you. If I don't take their help, my father gets insulted and threatens to cut me out of his will. When I do accept their money, my mother tells me where to spend it, and how I am supposed to feel about what she's told me to do. If I'm not successful in making money of my own, I'll never be free to live my own life. But the only ways I can be financially independent will make me just another cog in the wheel of their corrupt culture."

Isaac was terrified that if he chose the career that his parents expected, he would necessarily be miserable, just as surely as his acquiescing to family demands had determined his unhappy childhood and adolescence. The guidance given him by "overprotective, overindulgent, but mostly overwhelming" parents concerned decisions he would have been better off making for himself. He resented his mother and father's lack of respect for his judgment, but he had developed little confidence in any capacity for making his own correct decisions.

Isaac was frightened of becoming dependent on my direction, but he was also afraid that, if left on his own, he could never make it. Deeply depressed, he doubted every decision he made by himself and distrusted the motives of anyone who appeared willing to give him a hand.

Despite the fact that his obsessive analysis of every issue was depressing, both Isaac and I were relieved by his displays of wry and obscure humor. When he was not stuck in weighing the alternatives of talmudic "If on the one hand . . . , but then, on the other hand . . . ," his comedy was reminiscent of a curious combination of Groucho Marx and Samuel Beckett. For example, he once defined every career choice as akin to joining the Coast Guard. After leaving me bewildered for several moments, he went on to tell me what he meant was "it's unlikely to kill you, but it certainly can't get you anywhere."

Another time he declared that a writer whose name I'd never heard was his hero. After waiting long enough for comic timing, Isaac went on to explain that the writer he referred to was an obscure writer who had produced only nine short poems in seventeen years. Isaac could identify with him because "both our minds are mush; our words have lost all meaning; our only solutions are silence and absence."

When Isaac displayed signs of personal productivity, he saw them as dangerous acts of devotion to his destructive parents. While in therapy, he did odd jobs to defray expenses that his parents would have paid. But when he used his earnings to pay for a photography course, he became dismayed because some of his pictures turned out so well he was sure that if he showed them to his mother, she would like them. When he made remarks such as these, he was always "half-kidding, sort of."

I told Isaac of my own "paralysis" at about his age, when the graduate faculty in psychology unexpectedly accepted my dissertation proposal. Unable to betray myself by fulfilling the desires of my own intrusive parents who wanted me to complete my degree, for a year I was unable to attempt any further academic progress. Stuck in passivity and self-defeating defiance, once again I entered psychotherapy as a patient.

Whether or not it pleased my parents, I was determined to find a way to live a life of my own. Therapy helped some, but what meant even more was a visit from my father, against whose expectations my paralysis had been pitted. I was obsessed with both fear and hope that he would be devastated by my refusal to finish my dissertation and get my graduate degree.

To my utter amazement, somewhere in the opening exchange of his visit, my father inquired casually:

102

"Have you gotten your Ph.D. yet? I never can remember." Realizing that I had continued living in terror of a threat he had long ago lost interest in made it less of a threat to me as well. I had squandered an entire academic year at the mercy of a monster who turned out to be me. Isaac laughed in recognition of how this absurd account of my earlier madness reflected his own anguish.

Faced with awareness that he was already on his own, Isaac quickly back-pedaled to the treadmill of feeling trapped by financial dependence on his parents. If he did not continue in therapy, he would never escape his childhood fears and become truly autonomous. On the other hand, psychotherapy was a solution that simply recreated the problem. "So," he intoned, "as it turns out, my parents' paying for therapy gives them control over my life. And you, Mister Doctor of Psychology, believe if you analyze anything long enough, it will go away; by insisting on charging me so much money, you keep me inescapably tied to their apron strings."

In answer to Isaac's seemingly unresolvable paradox, I told him a simple story about myself: "Your situation reminds me of a dinner table exchange I had with my father when I was eighteen. For some reason that had nothing to do with me, he insisted that I accept ten dollars from him. I hadn't asked for the money, and I was in no position to repay it, so I told him, 'No thanks.' My father felt hurt and angry at my refusal of his 'gift.' Ten or twelve years later I experienced myself as very much on my own. I wanted to buy a house for my newly created family but didn't have enough money for a down payment. By then I was emotionally independent enough of my parents to feel completely comfortable calling my old man to ask him to give or loan me a thousand dollars."

Both Isaac and I were amused by the fact that by the time I told him the story, I could no longer remember whether I had ever repaid the money to my now long-dead father. Gradually Isaac began to realize that emotional freedom from his own intrusive parents was less a matter of financial independence than of actively attending to what he wanted for himself.

There were many emotional obstacles for Isaac to overcome. He feared that if he became as powerful and competent as he imagined his parents to be, then he too would be tempted to dominate people who depended on him. Paradoxically, he also believed that any belated effort to exist on his own would only serve to reveal that full disclosure of his peculiar personality would result in his confinement to the isolation of a back ward in some state mental hospital. Helpless to assert himself, once again he would find that he was deprived of personal freedom and forced to follow arbitrarily imposed institutional rules.

Although expressed in a form exaggerated enough to seem grotesque, Isaac's fears about personal power are much like those the rest of us feel from time to time. As children there were times when we felt so helplessly dependent that we were afraid we would never feel really grown up. It was then that we hid our anger from people powerful enough to destroy us for even imagining that we were entitled to feelings of our own.

At other times, we were afraid that we would grow up empowered enough to annihilate those big people to whom we had only pretended to defer. In some ways it's as scary to be a helplessly dependent child as it is to be a powerfully independent grown-up. Even as adults, there are times when we are so frightened that we don't feel very grown up, and other times when awareness of our adult capacity for becoming killers feels as frightening as a child's terrible vulnerability to being a victim.

Isolated by his fear of losing his identity, Isaac lived a lonely life of emotional distance from others. He com-

pensated for feeling inadequate in relationships by periodically proclaiming disdain for those who could not
match his own esoteric imaginings of a mathematical
meta-theory that would someday expose the meaning-
lessness inherent in social interaction of any kind. In
therapy, he admitted how unhappy he felt, bouncing
back and forth between an arrogant sense of superiority
over ordinary ignorant human beings, and a secret envy
of their apparent ease in relating intimately with one
another.

Isaac summarized this painful schism as his living "a
lunatic life immersed in mysticism one minute, and in
muck the next." More and more, his hollow boasts of
his "religio-aesthetic" interests began sounding (even
in his own ears) like the empty and pathetic protests of
a lost soul. It became increasingly evident that the appeal of algebra and calculus pivoted on providing inner
activities that did not require him to deal with other
people or "any other irrelevant emotional issues."

At first it was exceedingly difficult for Isaac to trust
that I was actually offering to help him discover what
might make his life happier. He could not believe that,
unlike his parents, I had no need for him to go to
graduate school, to become more outgoing, or to make
a lot of money. As he began to accept that I enjoyed
him as he was and wanted to help him change only
those things that he himself found upsetting, he decided
that we must both be the same sort of "kooks."

For a long while, however, he steered clear of dis-
closing the dreams and fantasies he found most frightening. Mainly, he talked of trouble in dealing with other
people. The cast of characters changed from time to
time, but the plot line was usually the same: Trying to
be a decent person who doesn't want to hurt anyone,
Isaac meets a new friend or lover. He sees that they
need his help, either to enlighten their traditionally conventional attitudes, or to rescue them from throwing

themselves away on jobs or marriages that don't suit their true needs. Each story ends in Isaac either giving up on their stubborn, shallow resistance to the help he has offered, or with their walking out on him because they mistakenly believe that he is unsympathetic and intrusive.

These stylized scenes gradually began to take on a more sinister aspect. Instead of understanding that the common themes in these relationships said something about his own style, he began to allude to secret meetings of "New York networks" between people who had nothing in common except that they had all betrayed him. New York was where his parents lived, and he believed the networks were some sort of "anti-intellectual terrorist conspiracy," but he would not tell me any more about it. It was clear that he was terrified that "they" would do him in, but he did not tell me how or why.

One day Isaac came to see me looking more worried, weary, and disheveled than usual. Uncharacteristically, he was silent for what seemed a long time. Finally I said, "You look as though you feel dreadful." After pausing a while as if deciding how much he wanted to disclose, he told me that the previous night he had had "another one of those nightmares." It was the first I'd heard of his dreaming at all. As if we had discussed the matter many times before, he insisted impatiently, "You know. That's why I'm so scared to go to sleep." His account of the nightmare follows:

I was somewhere dark and dangerous, but I felt so starved, I had to risk rooting around to find food. I was crawling on the ground when my hand touched what seemed like a small furry animal that I hoped was a rabbit. But when I stood up and raised it up to the light, it turned out to be the body of a dead rat. Its belly was so swollen that the skin had split

106

open. I could see its internal organs through a smooth, slimy membrane that was reddish purple and reflected what little light there was. It must have been dead for days. I wanted to vomit. I was about to throw it down in disgust, when I heard a snarl. A wild dog with terrible teeth made a lunge at the hand that held the rat. When I snatched my hand away to avoid getting it torn off, I ended up with rat in my mouth.

That was when Isaac woke up, scared to death that if he fell back to sleep he would dream that he "had to eat the rat."

I told him that some of my own *nightmares had turned out to be bad dreams only because I had been too scared to see them through to the end*. If he was willing to find out how this dream might have ended had he not awakened so soon, I would be willing to reenter the dream with him to give him a hand. Although the idea frightened Isaac, he was willing to give it a try.

Picking up where the dream left off, I asked him to try to shift his attention from what he feared might happen to what he wanted to do. After some alarm that he might end up eating the rat after all, with my support he decided that what he really wanted to do was to throw the dead rat to the ferocious dog, and for us both to get the hell out of there. I told him that was fine with me, but suggested that he take a moment more to see if there was anything else he wanted to accomplish before we made our escape.

Isaac acknowledged that before leaving, he might like to finish off the beast that had frightened him so badly. We looked for a way for him to destroy the dog. Isaac stumbled onto some rocks in the dream scene, but found them too heavy to lift and heave at the animal. I pointed out that if it was too hard for him to do the killing, he didn't have to, but if he wished, I would help him lift the rocks. He agreed enthusiastically, and together we did in the dog.

Once we had done the deed and fled the scene, I asked Isaac if he was still hungry. He said he felt starved and we set out to find him some food in his dreamscape. He came upon a patch of Brussels sprouts, a vegetable he said he'd always eaten and pretended to enjoy even though "I've always hated those green golf balls my mother made me eat. Because they were good for me, she insisted I was supposed to like the taste."

I told him that as far as I was concerned, he could eat them if he wished. Going on to point out that it was *his* dream, not mine or his mother's, I suggested that instead, he have some of whatever was his favorite food. He said he loved mushrooms but could find none on the dream scene. Under a tree with his initials carved on its trunk, I discovered some at once. Gratefully, Isaac accepted the mushrooms and ate them. Then he lent me his pocketknife so that I could carve my initials on a tree of my own.

After that session, although there were other nightmares on which we worked, Isaac reported sleeping better more of the time. He also let me know that for the first time he was learning to cook for himself, "whatever I want to eat." Over the next few weeks, grandiose elaborations on his esoteric mathematical theories gave way to proud descriptions of how quickly he had worked his way up from baking his first potato to making a pot of rice and beans.

Eventually there came a time when he talked about his longing to be known and loved. All of his life had been spent in emotional isolation, hiding his hunger for intimacy. I responded by saying, "You were frightened that if the family found out who you really were, they wouldn't let you live. But you managed to hide yourself so well that now you're afraid that no one will ever find you." For once in his life, my mathematical-genius patient was speechless.

Because I knew that the rest of his mourning could only come slowly, I allowed a long enough silence for Isaac to begin to experience the losses his isolation had cost him. Then I described the initial emergence of my grief over how much of my own life with other people had been lost to me.

When I was in my early twenties, I too had started out in psychotherapy as an impossibly intellectualized patient. I had complained that my therapist was so woefully ignorant about oriental philosophy that he would never understand me. He accepted my arrogant attack as understandable self-protection for someone as frightened as I was of feeling close to anyone. But, he went on to say, he thought that there might be much more to me than I could imagine in my philosophy. I had thought that my esoteric intellect was the only part of me I was permitted to claim openly as my own. I was touched by an unfamiliar feeling—that I might be a person anyone else might want to get to know better.

But recognizing this longing for contact suddenly made me afraid that all those years of intellectual obsession had been nothing more than an effort to avoid my dread of personal closeness. When I complained that this meant that I had lived a life empty of meaning, my therapist had smiled, and said: "Why not look at it another way? It could have been worse. If you had defended against your fear of closeness by an attack of hysterical blindness, your neurosis would have left you less prepared for intelligent conversation. Having defended yourself the way you did, if you ever feel safe enough to let someone know and love you, at least you'll be well informed enough for an intellectual discussion whenever you and your lover want to take a break." Remembering his response made me laugh and brought tears to my eyes.

Isaac also laughed at *the funny side of horror that comes with mutual disclosure*. Then he cried. We had both lived lives limited by attempts to hide out from our terror. For the moment, each of us stood before the other naked and afraid. Strangely enough, our being open to one another seemed safer than either of us had ever felt under the protective cover of our isolation.

# When It's Safer Being One of "Us," What Becomes of "Me"?

As our personalities developed, old fears resurfaced along the way. Each phase of our personal growth renewed earlier anxieties. Every time we were once again threatened with separation from protection, we felt tempted to turn back to our attachment to depending on familiar safe caretakers.

As if horror of being abandoned were not alarming enough, at times our renewed interest in further exploration of the unfamiliar echoed our earlier terror of the dreaded unknown. Faced with fear of finding the way on our own, we sometimes sought the security we'd known when we hid who we were.

At each new threshold, old anxieties and apprehensions reemerged. As children, we went off to school and had to make a place for ourselves in competition with others. When we entered adolescence, and then moved on into early adulthood, there were new uncertainties to be met. During each transformation, we were upset by echoes of the horror we abhorred as infants threatened with loss of our parents' protection, and by shadows of the terror that appalled us as toddlers exploring an unfamiliar world. Later we crossed the border into middle age and tried to make sense of what had become of the first half of our lives. When we entered our later years, we all confronted the alarming advent of our aging, the losing of loved ones, and the inevitability of our own deaths.

At transitional times of our lives, yesterday's horror of abandonment intertwines with today's terror of all that yet lies ahead. Each time we cross over into the next phase of our lives, we experience the renewal of familiar anxieties. Neither the seeming safety of earlier attachment to the protection of others, nor the illusory security of once again hiding who we are in isolation, seems sufficient to stem the tide of our old fears. During each new life crisis, once again the old dangers reappear.

Often the renewal of threats evokes a third strategy for coping with our fears. Once again we find ourselves so personally at risk we have difficulty accepting that *whatever fright we suffer in solitude is shared by everyone else*. Rather than face our fears on our own, we may wish to free ourselves of personal responsibility by merging with an anonymous communal identity. When we feel too scared to face our fears in person, we are tempted to seek the impersonal protection afforded members of social groups.

Instead of standing alone against fear, and counting only on the personal support of those who know us well, we assume the protective mantle of anonymous membership in nation, class, church, neighborhood, or ethnic enclave. Or we may define ourselves less as individual people than as representatives of the social roles we are assigned as physicians or factory workers, parents or adolescents.

Most of us make some communal mergers at various times and for a variety of reasons. In times of uncertainty they offer a kind of comfort. Some of us immerse our individual identities in the images of the groups to which we belong, but this security of merger with the communal "We" also entails unexpected risks to our individual "I."

Distracted for the moment from personal anxieties, we may take on the fears of the group. To our surprise, often we discover that coping with communal fears requires our unintended participation in social oppression. When our safety depends on joining the crowd, the group keeps who "We" are clear by excluding outsiders as "Them." We against Them, the majority against the minority, turns into good against bad, rich against poor, citizens against criminals, the sane against the crazies, and one generation against the next.

We pay a high price for safety sought in numbers. It is as though we cannot gather in groups to protect ourselves without feeling afraid that there is not enough good safe space to go around. If we are in, somebody else is out. Those the group excludes are deemed dangers to the community. We sound the alarm: "He (or she) is not one of us." Frightened that They want to do us in, we are out to destroy Them, or at least, to keep Them in their place. They just don't know what's good for Them; we do! Whether the others are welfare mothers, radicals, homosexuals, ignorant immigrants, or our own teenage kids, it's up to us to see that they don't do any harm.

Once we have established ourselves as part of the group, we must be careful to conform, or risk being banished as outcasts. If you're a true-blue American, you better not say anything sympathetic about godless Communists or illegal aliens! And if you want the support of certain conservative communities, you must not be permissive in raising your children. Paradoxically, in liberal groups, you can be branded as a bad parent if you do discipline your children.

Even when we do as we are told, the danger remains that we may be singled out arbitrarily and scapegoated for the greater good of the group. An outbreak of burglaries in our neighborhood makes everyone uneasy. When the community feels helpless to protect itself against outside harm, the majority may restore confidence in its power to cope with danger by blaming and punishing some innocent member of the group. "We never had any trouble before that new family moved in," they assure one another. "We need to let them know that their kind isn't welcome in our neighborhood. After all, we have to take care of our own. It's only right!"

This hypocrisy of social evil cloaked in apparent good is exquisitely illustrated in Shirley Jackson's superb story, "The Lottery."[1] Set in a typical small New England farm town, the story opens in the holiday atmosphere of an annual event, the Lottery. Villagers gather in the square on a sunny summer morning. Their acceptance of the occasion as a regular occurrence is evident in the "men's speaking of planting and rain, tractors and taxes."

When the women arrive, they engage in a quiet exchange of good-humored gossip. The girls stand aside and talk among themselves while the boys stuff their pockets with small stones and build a pile of larger ones in a corner of the square.

A subtle sense of tension prefigures the violence to come. The preparations for the ceremony begin with civic official Summers setting up a black box on a three-legged stool. The particulars of the ancient rite have largely been forgotten, the original box discarded, and paper slips substituted for the old wood chips. Mr. Summers stirs the papers in the black box and declares the Lottery open. The villagers are glad to get on with it so that they can be home in time for the noon meal, and then return to work.

As Mr. Summers reads the name of the head of every household, each man comes forward to draw a paper from the box. No one is to look at his folded slip until every family-head has had a turn. It is a ceremony that is held regularly in all of the surrounding villages.

During the drawing, the onlookers talk of the rumor that a nearby community is considering abandoning the practice. The critical comments of the crowd make clear that this is an almost unthinkable idea: "Pack of crazy fools listening to the young folks, nothing's good enough for *them*. Next thing you know they'll be wanting to go back to living in caves, nobody work anymore, live *that* way for a while. Used to be a saying about 'lottery in June, corn be heavy soon'; there's *always* been a lottery some places have already quit lotteries nothing but trouble in that pack of young fools."[2]

When all of the slips of paper are unfolded, word goes around quickly that Bill Hutchinson has "got it." Bill's wife Tessie protests that it is unfair. Her husband was not given enough time to pick any paper he wanted. The crowd shouts for her to shut up.

One of the other men asks Bill for the names of his three children. The Lottery official selects five slips to be put into the black box; one for Bill, one for Tessie, and one for each of their children: Bill Junior, Nancy, and little Dave. Each of the Hutchinsons takes a slip and in turn, each opens the folded piece of paper. The children open theirs first, and the crowd sighs with relief as each child displays a blank slip. Next Bill unfolds his slip, and shows them that his too is blank.

The crowd cries out that then it's Tessie who has won the Lottery, and instructs Bill to show them her slip. Dutifully, he forces the folded paper from his wife's clenched fist.

It had a black spot on it. Although the villagers had forgotten the ritual and lost the original box, they still remembered to use the stones. The pile of stones the boys had made earlier was ready. Tessie Hutchinson was in the center of a clear space. She held her hands out desperately as the villagers moved in on her. "It isn't fair," she said. A stone hit her on the side of the head. "It isn't fair, it isn't right." Mrs. Hutchinson screamed, and then they were upon her.[3]

When this fantastic tale of frightening folk customs first appeared, it evoked more shocked letters to the editor than any story previously published in *The New Yorker* magazine.[4] Readers expressed disbelief and denial of the violence exposed in the story. With the exception of a dozen appreciative letters from friends of the author, the hundreds of horrified reactions were all outcries of offended wide-eyed innocence.

Jackson responded to her audience's bewildered accusations and provocative abuse by jokingly proclaiming herself the only practicing witch in twentieth century New England. After the story had been anthologized, dramatized, and televised, fan mail became more polite, but much of the audience continued to insist that they could not understand what the story meant.

The writer's subsequent newspaper comment makes her own intent clear: "Explaining just what I had hoped the story to say is very difficult. I suppose, I hoped, by setting a particularly brutal ancient rite in the present and in my own village to shock the story's readers with a graphic dramatization of the pointless violence and general inhumanity in their own lives."[5] Confirmation is evident in the response of one reader who asked where the lotteries were held, and if the cruel ceremonial rite was open to the outside public.

"The Lottery" ends with the casting of the first stones. Jackson leaves the grisly details to our imagination. Up to that point, her characters seem so ordinary that their unexpected brutality catches us off guard. We are inclined to take the stoning for a crudely primitive practice, so anachronistically cruel that it appears alien to our own civilized equivalents.

But once we have finished reading this story, we are unable to escape an uneasy sense of frightening familiarity. On closer inspection we see the tale's similarity to social evils of prejudice and hypocrisy in our own contemporary communities. We still sometimes imagine that there is less than enough to go around of life's good fortune. This seeming scarcity makes us fear both our envy of others, and their envy of us. For safety's sake, someone must be sacrificed.

Yesterday's purification rite of sacrificing innocents can evolve into today's vigilante actions, in which evil is eradicated for the greater social good. Lynching is no longer allowed, but vigilante retribution is again on the rise, and social welfare programs are being wiped out. Ironically, some of the contemporary groups in which scapegoating remains most popular are made up of members of "the helping professions."

In a teachers' lounge I have heard underachieving students who misbehave denigrated as "delinquents who just don't want to learn." At a caseworkers' conference, I have heard multigenerational welfare families indicted as "irresponsible, hard-core cases." In psychotherapy seminars, I have often heard patients with whom little progress has been made accused of "resisting treatment."

*We blame the victims.* It's our way of feeling secure, learning that if our best efforts bring failure, we shall fear no evil because *it was not our fault.*

Therapists, caseworkers, teachers, and others who undertake caring for the needy usually start out trying to heal the unhappy, to speak for the voiceless, and to instruct the illiterate. When the going gets tough, many of us who started out as missionaries may be expected to begin blaming the natives. Some of us end up fearing and hating the innocent victims who bear our burden.

117

We discriminate between Them and Us because communal merger bolsters the belief that there is not enough good to go around, and exaggerates our fear that when one person or group gets something of value, others must do without. What's more, whenever we feel afraid that nobody can gain without someone else losing out, our panicky perspective arouses both the horror of unfulfilled longing, and the terror of being attacked because of the envy of others.

Envy itself is a form of fear arising out of the feeling that one person or group has more than another of whatever is desired. As protection against the envy and spiteful retaliation of both the gods and the neighbors, I was raised in the fearfully superstitious tradition of the Evil Eye. Any expression of admiration of another's good fortune or claiming of my own advantages had to be discredited by disclaimers.

Envy of modest gains could be easily warded off by intoning in Yiddish, "*kein einoreh*" ("may no evil befall us"). When others admired some advantage I had over them or if I boasted about it, I symbolically expelled its worth by spitting. By admitting that I had exaggerated I could diminish the danger; by complaining about some deficiency equivalent to theirs I could deflect any vindictiveness aimed at me. For example, if I or someone else commented that I was doing well at school, I would first ward off the Evil Eye by spitting, then by saying something like, "It was an easy exam, and besides, I'm never any good at athletics."

My grandparents brought over these communal pagan protective practices from their peasant village in the Old Country. I couldn't figure out how such superstitious folkways fit their Orthodox Jewish beliefs until I realized that one of the Ten Commandments might also allude to the Evil Eye.

The first nine commandments are all either injunctions against overt behavior, or instructions toward action. Only Number Ten (Exodus 20:17) refers to dangerous covert attitudes: "Thou shalt not covet thy neighbor's house, thou shalt not covet thy neighbor's wife, nor his manservant, nor his maidservant, nor his ox, nor his ass, nor any thing that *is* thy neighbor's."

Envy is a threat to the protection afforded by group cohesiveness. Exclusion by scapegoating and superstition restore the security of the homogeneous community.

My childhood recollections make contemporary superstitious protections against the fear of envy seem more ancient and alien than they turn out to be. Even in modern-day America, we knock on wood. Modestly, we may minimize our accomplishments by protesting that "it wasn't all that much," and whimsically invert our well-wishes about others who are approaching accomplishments of their own by telling them to "break a leg."

Superstition is only one of our communal ways of coping with the fear of envy. To maintain the security afforded by safely merging with a group, we must learn to obey its unwritten rules. We pretend to play down our competitiveness: When we win, we "don't rub it in," and if we are defeated, so as not to seem like "poor losers," we play down how much it may upset us.

Social conventions provide many ways of masking the anxiety implicit in envy. Sometimes group pressure makes it easier to commiserate with our neighbors' failures than to celebrate their successes. In most communities, bad news travels faster than good news.

Often, the price we pay for maintaining the morale of the group as a whole requires that we devalue the joy of any particular individual member. It is more acceptable to complain about obstacles in our way than to boast about how successfully we have overcome them. When we try something new, the group is less likely to trust that we will succeed than they are to

119

ridicule the failure they expect will result. Self-pity and chronic complaining may not increase popularity in the group, but both decrease the danger of being attacked out of envy.

That sort of modesty is not my style. I'm not much of a team player myself. Merger with a group has never been an easy alternative for me. I'd rather risk the envy of others and their vindictive attacks than stay safe by hiding my light under an umbrella of communal anonymity.

It's not that I don't ever get scared anymore. I often feel afraid. At times I recognize my anxiety as only an echo of my earliest horror of separation. Much of the time I realize that I will never be abandoned because of how awful I once imagined I was. Other times I can see that my present terror is only a shadow of an archaic fear for my life. It is reassuring to realize that I will not be destroyed simply because I have a self of my own.

Sometimes I still get scared even when I know there is no present danger. Unfortunately, not all of my fears are irrational. I have cause to fear failure, loss of people I love, disappointment, helplessness, and pain. And there is no doubt that I will sicken and die. On good days I fear that death will come too soon. After a string of particularly bad ones, I'm afraid it won't come soon enough.

But even when I have good reason to feel afraid, I'd rather risk facing it on my own than hide from my fear at the expense of sacrificing my scared self to a reassuring group image. I prefer revealing my envy of my sons' youth to hiding my personal fear of aging by playing the family patriarch and using them as emblems of my immortality. Whether within the family or in the world outside, to me the comforting company of someone else who also admits to being afraid feels better than joining a crowd of people who reassure one another that everything is going to be all right.

Despite my introverted eccentricities, there is one way in which merger with the group does ease my anxieties. So long as I am aware that *everyone* belongs to the group, accepting myself as one of the many can be a comfort. Some people may enjoy more advantages and others may be worse off, but everyone's most fundamental fears are the same. No one is safe from illness and injury, aging and death, or worry about the welfare of loved ones.

Whether we are writers or readers, early childhood experiences create our irrational adult fears. We must also take into account the communal contribution added by the time and place in which we grew up. Each culture and subculture has its own superstitious ways of coping with unwarranted fear of envy and other irrational anxieties, and each influences everyone who grows up in that particular community.

When my grandparents emigrated from Eastern Europe to America, packed among their meager material possessions were many small parcels of *shtetl* superstition that were not restricted to warding off the Evil Eye. Although my own family did not believe in vampires, they did hold that garlic cloves would cleanse our blood of evil urges and other impurities.

There were other family amulets as well. During an epidemic of infantile paralysis, my mother's mother sewed a cloth bag containing camphor and awful smelling herbs for each of her grandchildren. Until the danger of polio had passed, we wore these protective devices around our necks night and day.

Years later, as I became more skeptical, I questioned my grandmother's earlier attempts at immunizing us against that epidemic. Feigning humility, she shrugged and answered in Yiddish: "What does an ignorant old lady like me understand of such things? All I know is that not one of my grandchildren fell victim to that devil's disease."

121

In their aspirations to become assimilated "Yankees," my mother and father had also declared themselves free of the fears embedded in their own immigrant parents' belief in "greenhorn grandmothers' tales" and superstitions. Despite their claimed enlightenment, they pressured me to practice certain magically protective rituals. They did not truly believe in these rites, but they urged me anyway because "You never know!"

These practices included otherwise unacceptable behaviors such as spitting on the ground three times whenever I encountered someone stigmatized by an unusual physical deformity, dressed like a gypsy, or wearing Gentile clerical garb.

Superstition is a system of magical beliefs formed to fight our communal fear of the unknown. We protect ourselves against the impure powers that we project onto unfamiliar events and strange figures. We dread the difference between the ordinary and the alien because we exclude from our own image everything that we fear is evil.

At their best, superstitious fears and coping strategies serve to strengthen both our social sense of community and our psychological sense of security. At its worst, superstition encourages witch-hunts. Too often, as in the Inquisition, the process of saving deviants from their dreadfully unfamiliar differences destroys the damned whose salvation it has set out to serve.

Every era has its own superstitions. The Enlightenment excluded anything it could not explain. Romantic writers rebelled with Gothic novels, insisting that fear of believing in the uncanny was itself superstitious. My grandmother's freaks, gypsies, priests, and nuns were her equivalent of the Gothic novelists' monsters, ghosts, and undead vampires.

Someday I may question whether my current beliefs in depth psychology were nothing more than yesterday's superstitions. But while they work, like my grandmother, I shrug and answer, "Who am I not to believe."

Four

# Facing Fears and Easing Anxieties

# Through the Looking Glass

The mirror serves as a metaphor for reflecting the fears and anxieties that otherwise inhibit us from adventuring out to live life more fully on our own. It is an instrument of the imagination. Both in its capacity for contemplation of the self, and in its revelation of the universe, the looking glass is a mythic door through which the soul may pass to the other side. Nowhere is its inverted image more transparent than in Lewis Carroll's adventures of Alice in the wonderland that awaits our seeing through the looking glass.[1]

For more than a century these topsy-turvy tales of Alice's journey down and into the self have allowed us access to a captivating exploration of the uncanny underside of life. According to one writer:

In his mirror world Carroll replaces the normal left-right reversals of a mirror image to front-back inversions, time-reversals, and sense-nonsense reversals. Alice has to walk backwards to approach the Red Queen. Later, the White Queen explains the advantages of living backward in time and the Unicorn remarks, "You don't know how to manage Looking-glass cakes. Hand it round first, and cut it afterwards."

The king himself reflects this sense-nonsense inversion when he says that he wished he had eyes good enough to see Nobody.[2]

Children and grown-ups have consistently different reactions to Alice's unsettling encounters. Although these stories usually fascinate children, they often frighten them as well. Like Alice herself, most kids cannot accept the chaotic disorder of Wonderland that exposes life *as is*. Instead, they cling to the seeming security that there must be some personal reason for everything that occurs. ("The sun comes up early every day because morning is its favorite time.") When they visit Wonderland, their insistence on an ordered universe only makes them feel bewildered and powerless.

Most grown-ups, on the other hand, find that Wonderland gives us a chance to laugh at some of our absurd attitudes about the nonsense we encounter every day. As life keeps coming at us, there are times when we either learn to laugh at ourselves or we end up feeling frightened to death. As we look into our inner selves, the mirror's magical power of reversal reflects some things we wish we did not see. It takes a grown-up sense of humor to accept the horror hidden within each of us.

When we were very young, we experienced all parental actions and attitudes either as an intentional indictment of our being bad or as the rewards earned by being a good boy or girl. Nothing that happened was as yet experienced as accidental, or as an impersonal outcome indifferent to what we did or who we were.

When we were that young, understanding that a disapproving parent might be a person no child, no matter how perfect, could ever satisfy would have wiped out any hope for protection we might have had. Early on, we could not have faced knowing that at times the mother we depended on for survival was herself powerless to overcome the stress of illness, fatigue, poverty, and the like. An image of an indifferent or helpless mother would have been too overwhelming to be tolerated by anyone as small, as weak, and as dependent as we once were.

Rather than risk endlessly unfulfilled longing for an inaccessible protector, we blamed ourselves. By hiding whatever about us Mother seemed to experience as so awful, we protected our only hope of regaining her tender loving care. Unfortunately, the anxiety did not end there. Whatever we had to hide from Mother's disapproving eyes became buried and then unseen by ours as well.

As adults, those of us who are overly dependent remain uncertain about just what it is about us that's so awful that we still believe no one would put up with it. All we know is that often we cannot escape the unnamable horror that most people experience only occasionally: "If others knew what I'm really like, they wouldn't want to have anything more to do with me." To ease this anxiety, we must face our inner fears. When we first begin to look inside ourselves, holding up the mirror that fully reflects our horror is hard to do alone. If our overall confidence is only occasionally punctuated by moments of feeling afraid, talking with a trusted friend can reveal the hidden images that invite unnecessary anxiety. If our problems are pervasive, psychotherapy is the safest setting for discovering all that we have hidden for so long from others, and from ourselves as well.

This sort of self-examination is a little like the sharing of adolescent experiences. When I was a pimply-faced teenager, every boy in my crowd owned what we called "an ugly mirror." This hand-held, concave glass cruelly magnified every blackhead and blemish of the acne that indiscriminately blighted each of us.

The awful ordeal of scrutinizing the ugly eruptions

on faces we wished were attractive enough to appeal to neighborhood girls was easier to endure together than alone. Our only other alternative was to ignore the budding zits, and to risk that, untreated, they would bloom unexpectedly on a first date next Saturday night. It was better for us to know in advance of an appearance awful enough to invite rejection than to worry needlessly, or to be unprepared for an emergence that might have been avoided. In the company of accepting friends, it was easier to see our fears as funny, and to face them more squarely. After experiencing the absurdity of these experiences often enough in concert, it was less difficult to undertake them on our own.

As an example of how a psychotherapist can help someone to hold up their "ugly mirror" I'll tell you about a patient of mine I will call Patsy. She had been raised so intrusively that even as a very little girl, she had already begun to fear the danger of revealing that she had a self of her own. Her pietistically proper parents had pushed, poked, and prodded her. As a child she had been coiffed and costumed to be a porcelain and lace doll that they showed off to friends and neighbors. As much as she was able, Patsy passively complied with this dehumanizing transformation.

Unable to get her parents to attend to her inner needs, Patsy managed to set up a single isolated bastion of independence: she comforted herself by masturbating. To overcome this upsetting erotic holdout her parents took her to a child psychiatrist who they hoped would cure her of this "compulsive nastiness."

When I had reached an equivalent stage in my own delevopment, my parents consulted a pediatrician for advice about how to get me to outgrow my "incorrigibly disrespectful backtalk." Patsy and I enjoyed exchanging stories about our formative years. During those earlier times, I had thought that my name was "Shut Up!" She believed that hers was "Stop That!"

130

In one of our meetings, I was struggling to contain a cold with medication. My nose alternately ran, or dried up in reaction to the antihistamines I was taking. During a stopped-up, nasal dry spell, without awareness, I picked my nose.

Patsy was shocked that I would ever behave "so inappropriately." She told me that though she herself suffered from chronic allergies, during the many months we had been meeting she had felt afraid to blow her nose in my presence. I suggested she allow herself to imagine the danger she would have risked by exposing such unacceptable behavior. And, if she chose to accept my invitation, I urged her to exaggerate what the outcome might have been.

With obvious uneasiness, she told me: "I might not have stopped with just blowing my nose. Sometimes, when it was dripping snot, I might have wiped it on my sleeve. You would have seen how disgusting I really am. And you would have told me: 'Stop that, you nasty girl! Get out of my office, and never, never come back!'" Smiling, I answered, "It's no wonder that no matter how uncomfortable you felt, it was just too scary to take the chance of being blown away for blowing your nose. There would have been no way to protect yourself."

After a few moments of staid silence, an uncharacteristically mischievous grin lit up Patsy's usually prim face. Giggling, she allowed, "Well I guess I could have answered by telling you: "Shut up, you incorrigibly disrespectful character!' You wouldn't have thrown me out. We would have ended up laughing together".

That's just what we did. There were other fears to be faced, in both our relationship and in her personal life. But following that exchange. Patsy felt increasingly assured that she could safely endure more and more awareness and exposure of her own previously ignored inner needs.

Most of us are not all we pretend. Certainly, none of us is just what we were taught we were supposed to be. To the extent that our images of ourselves are incomplete, they are all misleading. Every personality is split. Each includes a full range of human capacities, both for all that is socially acceptable, and for all that is not. Whatever we wish to believe about ourselves, somewhere inside, the opposite is also true. Any awful things we may discover about ourselves need not be taken as an indication that this is who we "really" are. Our hidden wish to retaliate when hurt does not make brutality the core of our personality, nor do our "kinky" impulses imply that we are secret perverts.

For example, I may mean to say, "I want to *kiss* my wife," but make an inadvertent Freudian slip by saying, "I want to *kill* my wife." The psychoanalytic fallacy would have me believe that this slip means I really hate her unconsciously. Having already held up the mirror to what I feared I'd find in my heart. I am prepared to recognize my isolated hateful impulses. This awareness offers me the reassuring reflection of how much I love her, even though sometimes I certainly do feel like killing her.

Feeling scared is not the same as actually being in danger. In fact, it's often riskier to be caught unawares by unexpected exposure of what we fear than to become better prepared by intentionally meeting the beast where it lives. If we don't face our fear that secretly we sometimes hate the people we love, we increase the risk that without meaning to, we will hurt them badly.

At times we will find it useful to look through a glass darkly, and sometimes it is easier if we allow someone we trust to hold the magnifying mirror while we peer into the shadows. Using the metaphor of the mirror allows us clearer reflection of all that we are afraid lies within. Exposure of fearful secrets shared with friends who have equivalent anxieties may make our mutual fears funny enough to face.

Before mirrors were invented, primitives peered into the images that appeared on the still surface of natural pools. Despite the technological advancement of its modern manufactured artifact, the looking glass remains symbolically ambivalent. Looking into the mirror, we see right as left, here as there, and at times, we even see up as down and in as out.

In the service of our vanity, the looking glass flatters false images, but when we watch with careful, knowing concern, it reveals every flaw. The denials with which we mask our inner fears establish appropriately civilized public images of our modesty, gentleness, generosity, and reasonableness—all of which are too good to be true. *Peering into that inner darkness reflects a private person too true to be all that good.*

At times it may be worthwhile to display all these inflated virtues. But whatever the advantages of offering up an arbitrarily one-sided public portrait, not acknowledging our private vices is hazardous to our emotional health. Considerable tensions accompany the distrust and vigilance required to escape getting caught with our guard down. Although in some instances, it may be dangerously impolitic to make others aware of our darker desires, it is riskier still to hide them from our own inner vision.

Unless we break down the wall between outer propriety and inner perversity, self-improvements only serve as shallow resurfacing. Who among us has not had thoughts too crazy to admit, and impulses too cruel to confess? There are times when the best of us lie, cheat, betray other people, and belie higher principles. An expanded awareness of our shadow sides doesn't mean we have to act out every evil intention of our secret selves. A lack of awareness, however, leaves us at greatest risk, not only of experiencing needless anxiety, but also of acting out the impulses we fear most.

Maintaining responsibility for our unacceptable urges, and easing the anxiety they elicit in us, both require that we face our fears. Without flinching, we must be willing to look at the morbid and macabre mirroring of all we are that we wish we were not. Morality has no place in the imagination. In fantasy, everything is allowed.

It is not enough to take an occasional quick and cautious peek at the parts of our image we disapprove of. We must persist in peering deep into that inner darkness, with wide-eyed attention to our ruthless self-centeredness; or ravenous appetite for raw sensuality, our intense delight in the depravity we are tempted to indulge in, and our sweet savoring of the sadistic streak that is both deadly and delicious.

If we hold the mirror at an angle that flamboyantly exaggerates the sinister side of ourselves, our sinfulness appears as vivid as our more flattering conventional images. Only then does our savage hunger for the deviant, the strange, and the exotic emerge. In that dark light, we can see each evil aspect of ourselves as no more than a single side of a paradoxical illusion.

When we are willing to reflect with dreamlike decadence all that we usually cast out as "no, not that" and "that's not me," we don't have to fear coming on horror without warning. Without the old awful fear that anyone who really knew us could never love us, we can risk standing naked to the eyes of other people as well. In learning to live with the awful aspects of ourselves, we become more open to accepting them in others.

But the decadent imagination is not without its own dangers. Holding up that dark mirror opens us to the edge of madness, the risk of demonic possession, and to the pessimistic guilt that goes with acknowledgment of original sin. Most people seem to feel more secure imagining themselves socially proper and spiritually elevated. For myself, playing it safe and single-minded seems too high and too pure a path to be either interesting or earthy enough to be worth taking.

There are times when I so hate knowing how capable I am of indecency that I can no longer go on gazing at my own ghastly image. In the midst of disgust with myself, my courage leaves me. I turn away and resume dishonestly idealizing myself, insisting that I live a decent life only for its own sake. Secretly I am ashamed of how much I forbid my badness only out of fear of getting caught, and banished by those on whose care and protection I depend.

When I lack the courage to look at my own dark image in the glass, my world may seem safer and saner. But in the absence of that awful inner vision, my life lacks liveliness and passion. Whenever I am willing to recognize how often I hover somewhere between anarchy and madness, though I may feel scared, I'm never bored.

# Looking Evil in the Eye

The external counterpart of our anxiety about the horror of the dreaded darkness within is our apprehension of terror in the shadows around us. Just as turning the mirror inward confers confidence through acceptance of how awful we may be, turning the glass outward permits mastery over the unmanageably impersonal life situations that sometimes overwhelm us.

Whether in primitive superstitions, or in the up-to-date technology of telescopes, the mirrored reflections of distant images reveal the unknown universe. Following this model, the psychological looking glass is angled outward to telescope time by bringing closer our images of terror yet to come. By focusing on what we worry about as the worst things that might happen to us, we make the ominous, unknown future more familiar.

In myth and superstition, the mirror has long been used as a defense against outside dangers. Looking at Medusa's reflection in his shining shield, Perseus was able to slay her without staring at the serpent-haired head that would have turned him to stone. Merlin's magic allowed King Arthur's knights to observe their enemies without risking being seen. Like other amulets, mirroring objects have been used by primitives to ward off the Evil Eye.

Protection against outside threats afforded by the metaphorical mirror is not limited to baffling actual enemies or warding off evil spirits. The mirror can also be used to ease our apprehensions about whatever misfortunes may befall us. Accidents, injuries, illnesses, and criminal assaults are awarded indiscriminately. The external impersonal evil we must learn to live with is not delivered as punishment for sinners but rather as the undeserved suffering of innocents.

When the world around us seems filled with anticipated threats too overwhelming to understand, we are tempted to hide under the covers, asking only to be awakened when it's over. But our anxieties about unknown dangers do not go away when we are asleep. If we are unwilling to reflect upon them, they come upon us unexpectedly. Whatever scares us too terribly to be held up to the light will pursue us in our darkest dreams.

Our nightmares are chilling examples of the force of unfaced fears. At one time, people believed that terrifying dreams were caused by monstrously evil animal spirits. The "night-mares" were wild and unbridled phantom female horses that could crush the life's breath out of an innocent sleeper's chest. More recently, psychoanalytic theory has attempted to demythologize dreams by reducing them to defensively disguised fulfillment of forbidden wishes. Nightmares are then dismissed as dreams that unsuccessfully obscure anxiety associated with repressed sexual impulses.

From one era to another, the explanations change: first the supernatural, then the psychoanalytic, and next perhaps, the neurophysiological. But the map is *not* the territory. No explanation is sufficiently reassuring to transform a terrifying nightmare into "just a bad dream" which we need not fear. To ease our anxieties, we must hold up a mirror that will bring us close enough to the terror to let us experience all that we are tempted to keep at a distance.

137

Nightmares are more frightening than friendlier dreams because they are incomplete. When we use the daylight to dispel an unfinished dream, our avoidant behavior will be self-reinforcing. Absenting ourselves from one meeting with our dream-monster makes it even easier for us to miss the ending of our next nightmare.

There is a more productive way of dealing with nightmares. We have the option in the morning of mirroring last night's dream and following wherever it may lead us. When we do, we are less likely to wake up before the end of the next nightmare that previous avoidance invites. Continued attention to completing our dreams can even allow us to become aware that we are dreaming without having to waken.[1] Eventually we will be able to feel safe enough to explore our options while we dream.

Over the years, I have frequently pursued my own horrible fantasies to their conclusion (as I did with my patient Patsy's), and my personal nightmares to their end (as I did with Isaac's). The more I mirror my fears, the more I find my anxieties eased by completion of these dreaded dreams.

Recently I saw through to its end a nightmare meeting with impersonal evil. As background for describing that encounter, first I need to reveal more of my personal history.

I entered young adulthood in the early fifties. My career, courtship, marriage, and my hopes of having children all began during a terrifying era in America. Senator McCarthy's anti-Communist witch-hunt was scapegoating outspoken political innocents. I was about to be drafted into a non-war in Korea, confusingly called a "police action." The worst worry of my generation was our alarm about the atomic bombs that had needlessly decimated the civilian inhabitants of Hiroshima and Nagasaki.

138

My wife and I agonized over whether or not this was a time to bring children into the world. As yet unaware of the threat of total annihilation implied in what was then atomic warfare, we talked of moving to some safer place. In fantasy dialogues, we imagined relocating in New Zealand, in South America, or in some other setting so far from ground zero that it would be beyond danger.

The night of one particularly disturbing discussion, I dreamt that for twenty years we had hidden out in a cave in the Amazon jungle. After raising our children in the primitive protection of this remote cavern, we emerged to discover that there had been no atomic war after all. I woke up laughing at my exaggerated anxiety, decided to go on living in America, and raised three sons.

During the first years of our marriage, my career went well, and the kids grew up healthy. International armament build-up brought about increased tensions without ever exploding into a nuclear war. Unfortunately, in the meantime, unexpected catastrophic threats arose out of more personal contexts. All four of our parents suffered early deaths within a terrible three year period and then, at the age of thirty-eight, I was diagnosed as having a brain tumor.[2]

After three separate ordeals of neurosurgery and an intervening heart attack, I found myself emotionally battered, physically handicapped, and burdened with a poor medical prognosis. Renewing my willingness to survive beyond my initially suicidal solutions required that I face a life filled with terrible fears and awful uncertainties.

Accepting the unexpected outcomes of illness meant that I had to endure excruciating physical pain and crippling disabilities that earlier I would have imagined unbearable. At first the throbbing ache in my head was the worst of it. Headaches occurred often, hurt dreadfully, and lasted a long, long time.

Characteristically, I struck a stoic and heroic warrior pose, insisting that the force of my will would overcome any onslaught. But sheer willfulness worked no better than my inflated attempts at spiritual transcendence. Meditation, autohypnosis, and attempted escapes into recreational drug states all worked, but for too short a time. Codeine and other prescribed opiates partially eased my pain, but only in proportion to dulling the intuitive edge of alertness, and raising the risk of eventual addiction. Everything I tried worked for a while. Nothing I tried worked well enough to last very long.

Eventually I realized that if my agony was to be ameliorated, I had to face my fear and surrender to the hurting. Deliberately, I began to actively imagine what it might be like to live a life tortured by intractable pain. I hated yielding to the sight of myself so hopelessly helpless. But by indulging these awful fantasies, at least I was able to master imagining a frightening future that I had no other way of controlling.

Without insisting that I could overcome the fearful experience, each time the pain emerged I began to become increasingly able to accept its onset. After a while, an oddly detached curiosity made it possible for me to witness each new wave of pain without panicking over its never coming to an end. Ironically, I discovered that once the headaches were eased of the tension I had unwittingly added earlier by trying to fight off my fear of the pain, they hurt less!

The pain was further reduced by subsequent surgery, but only at the cost of impaired balance and diminished coordination of motor skills, each of which reawakened my panic. I became terrified of eventual paralysis. Unwilling to face how scared I was of someday finding myself trapped helplessly alive in a hopelessly dead body, I took on tasks I could no longer master. The anxiety I denied was unconsciously displaced into excruciating attacks of claustrophobia.

Whenever I found myself in a small enclosed space, I felt overwhelmed with alarm about ever again getting out. As long as I refused to accept the fact that I was partially crippled, and the probability of progressively debilitating handicaps, my worst fears were symbolically actualized in advance.

It was not until I accepted how frightening a future I might have to face that my needless claustrophobic terror abated. Once again, a scary story served me well. Remembering how chillingly claustrophobic I had felt, years before when I first read Poe's terrible tale titled "The Premature Burial," I deliberately decided to reread it.[3]

The story begins as a pseudo-scholarly account of actual cases of men and women who had been buried alive. Each was erroneously encoffined or entombed because of a state of suspended animation, misdiagnosed as death. Some were rescued, while others were later discovered who had apparently revived underground, only to then die of sheer terror.

Poe's journalistic narrative style catches the reader off guard. Only gradually do we realize that ghastly subjective details are insidiously woven into the seemingly detached objective accounts. Eventually, the narrator admits that he too suffers from catalepsy, a medical condition closely resembling death. When we read that he himself was once buried alive, we go into the grave with him.

When I reread this tale of terror I saw mirrored in it my previously unfaced fantasy of being buried alive. Facing that fear not only relieved my claustrophobia, but also reduced my well-warranted anxiety to a realistic concern about my actual prognosis. I then felt in my heart what earlier I had only thought in my head, that although I may be further debilitated by my tumor, I will never become completely paralyzed. This had been the neurosurgeon's prognosis which I had previously labeled as just another unconvincingly assuring idea. But when I nakedly surrendered to imagining the worst scenario I found comfort and reassurance in his clinical wisdom.

During the writing of this book, my wife and I had a dreadful dinnertime discussion about my illness and about how we were both nearing the ages at which our parents had died. We talked too about what we call the family's "revolving door," through which our grown children and their own young children periodically reenter the now cherished space of our life alone together. We needed time to talk about adapting to what had turned out to be the unkept promise of an empty nest.

A prodigal son had returned to recuperate from a misadventure. Two daughters-in-law redecorated the rooms of our house in preparation for the Christmas family gathering that now included four grandchildren. While excited about the holiday homecoming, I was also apprehensive about anticipated intrusions into the private sanctuary that my wife and I had established after the children left home. Talking with her about our very different styles of dealing with stress helped me to reset my emotional priorities by putting my excitement well ahead of my anxiety.

That night my dream started out in the awesome terror that a nuclear onslaught was in the offing. In the nightmare, my wife and I innocently assumed that we could survive the holocaust by staying in the house crouched down under heavy furniture.

An unstoppable storm of enemy missiles had already begun assaulting their targets. Watching through the windows, we saw our neighbors incinerated. Their houses and the surrounding woods were turned to ashes. Our world had collapsed.

Knowing that we needed to seek safer refuge, we

sorted out the supplies we would need to take with us for survival. Recognizing my dreaming self as old and ill, at first I concentrated on gathering hearing-aid batteries and painkilling medications. As soon as I realized that much of what had seemed valuable was not worth taking along, I set aside money and "important" papers, and substituted comfortable boots, a Swiss army knife, and food compact enough to carry in my backpack.

After a time, our elaborate preparations gave way to the urgency of just getting going. Once on the road with other refugees we saw their suffering and became aware of the likelihood that none of us would make it to safety.

The dream ended with a transforming revelation that stayed with me beyond my awakening to the relief of morning light. I realized that, whatever our terror, all that really mattered was was that my wife and I continue our journey together, that we willingly walk the refugee road, and that WE CARE FOR ANY OTHER FRIGHTENED CHILDREN WE MIGHT MEET ALONG THE WAY!

# Epilogue

During the early years of his final incarnation as a young prince, the Buddha's family protected him from ever encountering illness, aging, or death, and so he did not yet know what it was to be afraid. After a long while, he finally saw an old man, a sick man, and a corpse. When he witnessed these dreadful dangers, he would not turn away in fear. Instead he spent his life searching for some way of freeing people from the attachments that keep us trapped on the wheel of life's sorrows.

After years of pursuing other paths, he seated himself under the Tree of Englightenment. There he practiced the meditations that would take him to the threshold of release from fear and other forms of suffering.

It was then that the Evil One, Mara, tried to tempt him. Hoping to evoke envy in the Buddha, first Mara sent his dancing daughters: Lust, Greed, and Ambition. Next he appeared himself to invite Buddha to give up his austerities and accomplish great works in the world. But when the Buddha grounded himself by touching the earth with his hands, this *mudra* diminished the Evil One's impact until he was like a crow attacking a rock.

Next Mara tried to distract Buddha's attention by assaulting him with terrible armies of dark and devouring monsters. They appeared in a mighty storm of live coals, hot ashes, and boiling mud. Again the Buddha sustained his safety with a *mudra*, this time by raising his right hand against fear.

In desperation, the god of death and desire then tried to tempt him to accept at once the protection from pain and suffering he had already attained. But Buddha extended his other hand in the *mudra* of compassion, and announced his decision to go on facing his fears in this life so that the protection of his understanding would remain available until the last of us had also attained enlightenment.

# Notes

## Prologue

1. Dale E. Saunders, *Mudra: A Study of Symbolic Gestures in Japanese Buddhist Sculpture*, vol. LVIII of the Bollingen Series (New York: Pantheon Books, 1960).

## Chapter 2

1. Susan Cunningham, "The Public and Nuclear Power," *American Psychological Association Monitor* 16 (February 1985), 1ff.

## Chapter 3

1. Heinrich Zimmer, *The King and the Corpse: Tale of the Soul's Conquest of Evil*, ed. Joseph Campbell (Princeton, New Jersey: Princeton University Press, 1957).

2. Ibid., 213–214.

## Chapter 4

1. *The Teachings of the Compassionate Buddha,* ed. E.A. Burtt (New York: Mentor Religious Classics, New American Library, 1955), 44ff.

2. Mary Shelley, *Frankenstein: Or, the Modern Prometheus*, with an afterword by Harold Bloom (New York: A Signet Classic From New American Library, 1965). [First published in 1816.]

3. Bram Stoker, *Dracula*, with an introduction by George Stade (New York: Bantam Books, 1981). [First published in 1897.]

4. Robert Louis Stevenson, *Dr. Jekyll and Mr. Hyde*, with an afterword by Jerome Charyn (New York: Bantam Books, 1981). [First published in 1886.]

5. Dr. Polidori's short story, "The Burial," was later expanded into a vampire novel that eventually served as a model for Stoker's *Dracula*.

6. Shelley, x-xi.

7. This is not to mention the expression of deep, subconscious fears of sex and childbirth which many scholars read into Shelley's work. In other words, the "nightmare" she actually lived—only one of her several pregnancies resulted in a child who lived to adulthood—may also come to life in *Frankenstein*.

## Chapter 5

1. Edgar Allan Poe, *The Best Known Works of Edgar Allan Poe: The Best of the Famous Tales and Poems* (Garden City, New York: Blue Ribbon Books, 1941).

2. Ibid., 267–280.

## Chapter 6

1. Flannery O'Connor, "A Good Man Is Hard to Find," in *A Good Man Is Hard to Find and Other Stories* (New York: Harcourt Brace Jovanovich, Publishers, 1976), 9–29.

2. In treating O'Connor's story solely as a tale of terror, I have deliberately avoided attending to the richly rewarding religious aspects of her writings, about which so much has been written elsewhere.

3. William F. Allman, "The Compleat Worrier," *Science* 8 (October 1985): 36.

## Chapter 9
1. The mothering person need not have been either a biological parent, or even a female.

2. William Faulkner, "A Rose for Emily," in *Collected Stories of William Faulkner* (New York: Random House, 1950), 119–130.

3. Ibid., 130.

## Chapter 10
1. Eudora Welty, "Clytie," in *The Collected Stories of Eudora Welty* (New York: Harcourt Brace Jovanovich, Publishers, 1980), 81–90.

2. Eudora Welty, "Place in Fiction," in *The Eve of the Story: Selected Essays and Reviews* (New York: Random House, 1970), 128.

3. Eudora Welty, *One Writer's Beginnings* (Cambridge, Mass: Harvard University Press, 1984), 104.

4. Welty, "Clytie," 90.

5. Welty, "Clytie," 90.

## Chapter 11
1. Shirley Jackson, "The Lottery," in *The Lottery: The Adventures of James Harris* (Cambridge, Mass: Robert Bentley, 1980), 291–302.

2. Ibid., 207.

3. Ibid., 301–302.

4. Shirley Jackson, "The Lottery," in *The New Yorker*, June 26, 1948, 25–28.

5. Lenemaja Friedman, *Shirley Jackson* (Boston: Twayne Publishers, 1975), quoted in the *San Francisco Chronicle*, July 22, 1948, 64.

## Chapter 12

1. Lewis Carroll, *The Annotated Alice: Alice's Adventures in Wonderland & Through the Looking Glass*, illustrated by John Tenniel, with an introduction and notes by Martin Gardiner (Cleveland and New York: Forum Books, The World Publishing Company, 1963).

2. Benjamin Goldberg, *The Mirror and Man* (Charlottesville, Virginia: University Press of Virginia, 1985), 242–243.

## Chapter 13

1. Stephen LaBerge, *Lucid Dreaming* (Los Angeles: Jeremy P. Tarcher, Inc., 1986).

2. Sheldon Kopp, *Here I Am, Wasn't I!: The Inevitable Disruption of Easy Times* (New York: Bantam Books, 1986). This is the most recent of my repeated accounts of these ordeals. These writings help me face the fears I meet along the way.

3. Edgar Allan Poe, "The Premature Burial," in *The Best Known Works of Edgar Allan Poe: The Best of the Famous Tales and Poems* (Garden City, New York: Blue Ribbon Books, 1941), 290–299.

# About the Author

SHELDON KOPP, Ph.D., is the author of many popular and visionary books. He is a licensed psychologist and George Washington University Associate Clinical Professor Emeritus of Psychology, with "many scars but no tatoos."